DADDY'S GIRL

Living as God's Beloved Daughter

LANNA ANDERSEN

ISBN 978-1-0980-9124-8 (paperback)
ISBN 978-1-0980-9125-5 (digital)

Christian Faith Publishing, Inc.
832 Park Avenue
Meadville, PA 16335
www.christianfaithpublishing.com

Printed in the United States of America

To my husband, Brandon. You're a great dad.
And to Pastor Mark. You've taught me everything I know.

Contents

Introduction

Twelve years ago, my pastor was preaching a sermon series on prayer in which he explained that talking to God is a lot like a little kid talking to their daddy—freely, frequently, and with warm affection. My initial reaction was, "That sounds wonderful, but I have no idea how to do that." In the following days, as I continued to think and pray about the concept of talking to God like He's my dad, the Holy Spirit very clearly showed me three things: I didn't know what this kind of tender father-daughter relationship was like; I carried a deep wound left by my earthly dad; and I desperately wanted to know God as my Father. I felt overwhelmed and had no idea where to start to untangle what felt like a mess of hurt, emotions, fears, and misconceptions.

A few weeks later, my pastor's wife was kind enough to meet with me to talk over these new things God had revealed. We talked, cried, and prayed together. She was patient with me and let me verbally process my thoughts, fears, and hurts. And the singlemost helpful piece of advice she gave to me was not to focus on fixing the problem but to focus on God and getting to know Him as my Father. He alone would be my source of love, comfort, truth, healing, strength, and peace. And she was right. That day began my journey of getting to know God as my Father. Like with many relationships, that journey has at times proceeded in fits and starts. Sometimes it feels as if I take three steps forward and two steps back. Yet He's been there with me the entire time, being patient with me as I learn to trust, receive, and rest in His love.

A few years later, as I driving my minivan on a random weekday, running errands, I became lost in thought about my relationship with God and how far we had come. The Holy Spirit spoke to me very clearly once again about God the Father:

> Some dads abandon their daughters, but your heavenly Father will never leave you.

> Some dads lie to their daughters, but your heavenly Father always tells the truth.

> Some dads are dark, but your heavenly Father is always and only light.

> Some dads harm their daughters, but your heavenly Father wants to heal you.

The list went on and on. I wasn't even thinking. It was as if a dam had broken loose, and these words flowed into my mind and heart. I knew these truths came from God's Spirit and gave words to what I had been thinking and feeling. I later wrote the truths God gave me that day in a blog post in which I provided scriptures for each truth about the Father. The response from readers shocked me. Women came up to me at church, sent emails, and commented online that seeing the truth of who God the Father is contrasted with how their earthly dads treated them was nothing short of eye-opening. Too often we project the character of our earthly dad onto God. If our dads abandoned, abused, rejected, or neglected us, we fear that God might do the same. Sometimes this fear becomes so great that we reject God altogether.

I am thankful that God used that blog post to help many women, but one blog post of a thousand words can only accomplish so much. Clearly many women have a father wound and need to know God as their Dad. So I expanded that blog post and wrote this book. Before we get going, I want you know what God has laid on my heart as I've written this book.

First of all, I am not writing from a place of expertise but rather from a place of experience. I needed this book myself. The time that I have spent with God in Bible study, prayer, and struggle at my laptop have built my relationship with Him far more than I ever dreamed. I have not only learned about the character of God the Father, but I have also learned how to be His daughter. I have learned to love Him, to trust Him, and to let my guard down with Him because He is safe, loving, good, and faithful. My hope and prayer is that you, too, will find your Father as we search His Word together.

Second, for many years I thought I was just one of those women who had "daddy issues." I had learned to live with the pain, and I didn't think it was a big deal. Let me tell you, "daddy issues" are a big deal. If you have any unforgiven, unresolved, unhealed hurt from your relationship with your earthly dad, you have a father wound. It has been said that the most important things about us are who we think God is and who we think we are. It follows then, that if our dads distorted our view of God as a Father, this will affect every area of our life. A father wound doesn't simply go away with time. It can only be healed by spending time with your Heavenly Father.

Third, my intention is not to throw gasoline on the fire if you have a father wound from your earthly dad. I don't want to inflame any hurt, anger, or bitterness you may feel toward him. Even so, we need to see the reality of how our dads may have negatively impacted our lives, whether intentionally or unintentionally, in order to heal and move forward. As Christians, we often talk about the freedom we have in Christ. Yet in my own life, I haven't been able to move forward in freedom until I experienced deliverance from the pain that was chaining me to the past. God can heal that pain.

Fourth, I do not want create problems where there are none. If your dad is a godly man and you have a good relationship with him, praise God for that! You can still learn from this book more about who God the Father is and how He feels about you. Perhaps you'll even see new ways in which your dad showed you what the Father is like and you can thank him for that. Even if you don't have a personal father wound, I'd be willing to bet that you can name a few women in your life who do. My hope is that this book would help you grow in compassion for them and give you some things to share with them about God the Father.

Fifth, my desire is that the Holy Spirit will help you start to figure out and articulate if there are lies you believe, if there are hurts you carry, and if there are fears you have that stem from how your dad may have treated you. I want you to get to know God as your Father and trust how He feels about you. I want you to forgive your dad and allow the Holy Spirit to renew your mind about who God is. I know this seems like a lot. It will be a process, but we'll take it one step at time. God will be patient and tender with you as He has been and continues to be with me.

Sixth, my goal is to be helpful. I am not a theologian; and this book is not a comprehensive, systematic study of God the Father. This is also not a book that will simply declare affirmations over you. Positive thoughts and cheerleading are not enough to heal the soul. We will have to delve into some uncomfortable places, perhaps even some memories you'd care not to relive. But that's where the healing comes from; and with God's help, I know you can handle it. I've found that however deep a wound is, God's healing runs even deeper.

Finally, this is not a man-hating or dad-bashing book. Our culture is intensifying its dismissal, disrespect, and demonization of men. Our culture also demeans their significance in the lives of children, as leaders of the family, and as pillars of society. So instead of joining culture in berating, belittling, and battling against men who have hurt us in our past, let's allow God to heal our father wounds so we can help build men up and change the future, starting with our husbands and sons.

I began my journey to get to know God as my Father over ten years ago. It has been a process full of fits and starts, times of stagnation, and times of miraculous revelation. I understand that what I'm asking you to do may seem scary and insurmountable. As I said, when I realized that I had a father wound, I had no idea where to start. That's why I hope and pray you'll trust me to lead you lovingly through the pages of this book. More than that, I hope and pray that you'll trust God. I have been where you are now, and I can tell you this: whatever it may cost to wade through your father wound is worth all the healing that you'll find on the other side. Although I'm still learning and growing closer to God the Father, let me encourage you with what I now know to be true:

> I know the pain an earthly father can inflict.

> I know that you do not have to continue to carry this pain.

> I know that God the Father can heal the wounds left by your dad.

> I know that He is indeed a Father to the fatherless.

My prayer is that you'll go on this journey with me through the Bible and see God the Father for who He truly is. I pray that you will feel His healing love deep in your soul in that part of you that still feels like a little girl who just wants a dad. You've got One, the best One there is. I can't wait for you to get to know Him.

PART 1

Distant Dads

1

God Is a Father Who Works through Fathers

In the Christian faith, there is a complicated and mysterious belief that God is one God who exists in three distinct persons—God the Father, God the Son, and God the Holy Spirit. We call this three-in-one God the Trinity. When my husband was a kid, he called each of these the mean one (Father), the nice one (Jesus), and the weird one (Holy Spirit). Many Christians feel more comfortable talking about Jesus or the Holy Spirit than the Father. Those of us from an Evangelical background tend to focus more on Jesus, and those of us from a charismatic background tend to focus more on the Holy Spirit. As a result, many churches today either minimize or entirely neglect to teach and talk about God the Father. I am in no way arguing that we ought to dial down the importance of Jesus or the Holy Spirit, but I am suggesting that we dial up the importance of God the Father. I'll show you why.

Jesus is crucially important, as He's our only option for salvation and forgiveness of sin. But what did Jesus care about? What did He say He had come to earth to do? Jesus Himself said that He came from the Father to show us what the Father is like, that He was the way to the Father, and that He came so that we could be together with them.[1] Jesus came to do exactly what the Father had asked Him to do and never deviated from His mission. Part of Jesus's mission

---

[1] See John 14:1–11.

was to show us how to have a personal father-child relationship with the Father. In the book of Galatians, the apostle Paul declares, "Grace to you and peace *from God our Father* and the Lord Jesus Christ, who gave himself for our sins to deliver us from the present evil age, *according to the will of our God and Father,* to whom be the glory forever and ever. Amen" (emphasis mine).[2] The salvation that Jesus made possible for us was God the Father's idea, so we can't only focus on Jesus.

In the same way, we need to be mindful of overemphasizing the Holy Spirit to the neglect of God the Father. The Holy Spirit plays a crucial role in the life of every Christian because He is the one who convicts us of sin and draws us to Jesus. God's Spirit dwells in us and helps us to put others' needs above our own, to say no to temptation, and to understand the scriptures. He also works through us to resist the schemes of the enemy and to walk in the victory Jesus accomplished on the cross. While we do need the Holy Spirit to empower us to live a godly life in an ungodly world, if we overemphasize the Holy Spirit and neglect the Father, we cut ourselves short. Galatians 4:6 (NLT) says, "And because we are his children, God [the Father] has sent the Spirit of his Son into our hearts, prompting us to call out, 'Abba Father!'" God the Father sent the Holy Spirit to dwell in our hearts to enable us to cry out, "Daddy! I need you!"

God the Father, Son, and Spirit are three distinct persons but one in essence, and we cannot separate them or give one more importance than the others. Though it's not a perfect analogy, we can think of the Trinity as a family made up of God the Father, God the Son, and God the Holy Spirit. God is in Himself an unending, unbreakable, unbounded relationship of love, joy, peace, and closeness. God the Father is the head of this family, and this is the family that He invites each of us into. Yes, the Trinity is hard to understand—a mystery we won't fully be able to understand in this life on earth. A children's app that I like which we use in our house explains that the Trinity is "three in one" kind of like three sides on a triangle, three leaves on a clover, or three blades on a windmill. These pictures show

---

2   Galatians 1:3–5

us something of what God is like: one God in three persons, one yet three.

In order to have a full, thriving relationship with God, we need to have a relationship with all three persons—Father, Son, and Spirit. The Father sent Jesus as our Big Brother to earth to show us what He is like and to bring us back into His family. God the Father also sends His Spirit to dwell in every believer to empower them to love God and live for Him. So then, we must continue on the journey to get back to the Father's side, for that is what both Jesus and the Holy Spirit help us to do. The Father's side is where, as God's children, we were intended to be all along. It is only with Him that we find the healing and wholeness that every person on earth is looking for. Let's now take a look at what exactly God means when He calls Himself Father.

What Is a Father?

Our culture today has many definitions of what a father is. Some say a father is simply the man who impregnated the mother of his child. Other people say your father is the man who raised you, fed you, and taught you about life. Still others say a father is the one who sends child-support checks, criticizes everything you do but never admits his own faults, or the one who glares at your date when he arrives to pick you up. An adoptive father, stepfather, or spiritual father sometimes fills the role left by a biological father. Some of these descriptions are positive, but many are decidedly negative. Our culture has no singular definition of what a father is because it doesn't understand who God the Father is. God could have revealed himself using any title He wanted; and in relation to His people, God chose to call Himself Father. He chose a relational word because God, by His nature, is relational. To find out what God means when He calls Himself Father, let us go to Bible and see what God says about Himself.

The word most commonly used for *father* in the Old Testament, which was written in Hebrew, is the word *ab*.[3] It does in fact mean what you probably assume it means: "a father of an individual, an ancestor, a head of household." But as with many Hebrew words, it means so much more than an English translation indicates. This word *ab* also tells us how a father is to act: he is to be a provider, a benevolent protector, a teacher who brings up and nourishes his children and is connected to them in intimate relationship. God uses this word *ab* for Himself as well:

> Father to the fatherless and protector of widows is God in his holy habitation. (Ps. 68:5)

> But now, O LORD, you are our Father; we are the clay and you are our potter. (Isa. 64:8)

So we see that by calling himself Father with this Hebrew word *ab,* God intends for us to not view him as the angry Old Testament guy in the sky but rather as a tender, loving, protective, and faithful Father who desires to have an intimate relationship with us. Contrary to common misconceptions, God the Father in the Old Testament is not a harsh dictator ruling nations from afar but a loving Father who chose to work through fathers—men like Abraham, Isaac, Jacob, and Joseph—to create families who love Him. These were not perfect men, but they were men who had a perfect Father.

The image that comes to my mind when I consider this type of a father is bedtime in my house. The process of getting four kids ready for bed begins in total chaos. "It's like herding cats," as my husband says. But once everyone is in their pajamas, teeth are brushed, and school clothes are laid out for the morning, the mood transitions. My husband puts our three daughters to bed while I put our son to bed in the adjacent bedroom. Through the wall, I hear Bible stories being read, talking, laughing, conversations about the girls' days at school, plans for the weekend, and prayers for no bad dreams.

---

3   Tregelles, Samuel Prideaux. *Gesenius's Hebrew and Chaldee Lexicon.*

I am so grateful that my daughters know what an *ab* kind of father is. God is a Father like this: tender, attentive, loving, and secure.

Whereas the Old Testament refers to God as Father in relation to the nation of Israel, Jesus came on the scene in the New Testament and changed all that. "Jesus, in fact, shocked and offended the religious leaders of his day by claiming he had a Father/Son relationship with the God whose name they feared even to pronounce. Furthermore, by inviting his followers to call God 'Father,' he made this the primary name by which God is to be known to his followers."[4] In fact, Jesus referred to God as his Father over 175 times in the Gospels. Predominantly written in Greek, the word most commonly used for father in the New Testament is *pater*. It comes from the root word *pa,* which literally means nourisher, protector, upholder.[5]

I loved to watch *Little House on the Prairie* as a little girl. The show, which is based on a series of books by Laura Ingalls Wilder, follows the Ingalls family and their life on the American frontier. Charles, their *Pa,* was what I dreamed a dad could be like. He was strong, protective, resourceful, and always had plan of where he was leading the family. Yet he was also tender with his wife, Caroline, and their children. I remember watching Pa walk into their tiny log cabin after a full day of farm labor or working at the town sawmill and bringing life into the home. He would devour whatever Ma had made for dinner—no doubt made from very simple ingredients— like it was a Christmas feast. He would often play a happy tune on the fiddle around the roaring fireplace while the children danced and giggled. Pa had an infectious laugh and the most joyous smile. I actually remember riding in the car one day when I was ten years old and news came on the radio that Michael Landon, the actor who played Pa, had died. I felt a surprising stab of sadness. I obviously understood that it was the actor who had died, not Pa himself. Nevertheless, Michael Landon as Pa was my idea of what a father was like, and I felt sad that he was gone.

---

4   Spangler, Ann. *The Names of God: 52 Bible Studies for Individuals and Groups,* 125.
5   *Thayer's Greek Lexicon, Strong's NT* 3962

When we take all of this together, both the Old Testament and New Testament words for *father*, we discover this: a father is the head of the family who takes responsibility for creating, nourishing, protecting, guiding, and upholding his children with love, kindness, and affection for the sake of his children's good. This is who God the Father is and who He intends for earthly fathers to be. By calling both Himself and dads on earth by the same name, God is expecting that earthly fathers will mirror His character (albeit imperfectly) to their children. God the Father is the head of the Trinity, and He created fathers to be the head of the home, taking responsibility for the nurturing of the family.

Dad Distortions

Unfortunately, instead of helping us to understand what God the Father is like, many of us have earthly dads who clouded or distorted our view of Him. There are three general "dad distortions" that I have observed, both in my own experience and having been in ministry for over ten years.

Distant dads. Some dads are physically distant. These can be dads who abandon their kids, see them only on weekends or holidays, or dads who have never even met their kids. Sometimes dads aren't intentionally distant, but perhaps they have died or are away for long periods of time due to work or military service. Though the distance is not intentional, it can still negatively affect a dad's ability to have a close relationship with his children.

It is possible that a dad is physically present but emotionally distant. These dads don't pursue relationship with their kids despite having the opportunity and ability. When life gets tough, they pull away, or they allow issues to come between them and their kids. Emotionally distant dads sometimes give their children the silent treatment instead of talking through difficult situations. Oftentimes as well, dads become emotionally distant as their daughters enter puberty and become young women, no longer sure of how to interact with them. A common result of having a distant dad is becoming a daughter who says, "I'm fatherless, but that's okay. I've learned to deal with it." The problem is compounded if we become a daughter who also says, "God—if there even is one—feels distant, but that's okay. I'm fine on my own."

Destructive dads. These dads are mean, overbearing, controlling, and sometimes violent or abusive. Destructive dads sometimes have unrealistic expectations or make their children earn their love and approval. These dads can also be good at giving rules but bad at growing a relationship. Sometimes these dads appear very religious but are not very relational. A destructive dad can lead us to project onto God the Father a harshness and capriciousness that He doesn't possess. We begin to believe that God is a ruler in heaven who merely wants us to obey His commands or that He cares more about what we can contribute to His kingdom than who we are as His daughter.

Delicate dads. These dads are often weak. They frequently abdicate their responsibility to lead their family and defer to mom in such important areas as raising the children, discipline, and finances. They can also be selfish, foolish, immature, and not respectable. They can be dads who are shortsighted about the future; they care more about having a good time than investing in their kids and creating a good legacy. They are dads who don't teach their kids about life or protect them as they venture out into the world. You might feel loved by his tenderness but unloved by his lack of protection and leadership. A delicate dad can lead us to develop a liberal view of the Father, in which we perceive His attitude to be "live and let live." We can wrongly believe that God just wants us to just be happy and that He's more of a friend than a parent.

It is important that we pay attention to ways that our dad may have distorted our view of God the Father because we tend to either *project* our dad's character onto God or *reject* Him entirely. We cannot have a healthy, close, tender relationship with the Father unless we see Him for who He truly is. In addition, identifying potential dad distortions is important because we tend to drag these distortions into our marriage and relationships with other men, particularly men in authority (i.e., political leaders, pastors, professors, etc.).

Some dads really do try their best. Yet even the most godly of dads are still human and will at times fall short of being the kind of father that God is. The point of recognizing these dad distortions is not to denigrate our dads but to grow our relationship with God by seeing Him for who He truly is. We'll explore all of these dad distortions in the following chapters through the stories of real women.

Our Great National Crisis

While I want you to personally encounter God as your Father in the pages of this book, I also want you to see that this issue of fatherlessness is an epidemic in our nation. It is perhaps our greatest national crisis yet is seldom talked about. Behind this issue of fatherlessness is a spiritual battle wherein Satan is attacking the core issues of humanity and how God designed life to work. The truth is that God is in charge. We are His rebellious kids who have been provided rescue and adoption through Jesus, and we are to model our lives and families according to His perfect, loving ways. What the enemy wants you to believe is that you are destined to keep the father wound you currently have and it is not possible to have the dad you long for. That, my friend, is a demonic lie. You do have the dad you long for in God the Father. This battle over the issue of fatherhood is a battle of life versus death, truth versus lies, light versus dark, love versus hate, and peace versus chaos. It is a battle between the God who made you and loves you and the enemy who wants to steal, kill, and destroy everything that God intends for your life. You may think I'm overstating the impact of father wounds, but the statistics back me up.

The National Fatherhood Initiative declares, "There is a father absence crisis in America. According to the U.S. Census Bureau, 19.7 million children, more than 1 in 4, live without a father in the home:

This represents children living without a biological, step, or adoptive father.[6] Consequently,

---

6   Source: 2017. U.S. Census Bureau. https://www.fatherhood.org/fatherhood-data-statistics

there is a father factor in nearly all social ills facing America today. Research shows when a child
is raised in a father-absent home, he or she is
affected in the following ways:

- Four times greater risk of poverty.
- More likely to have behavioral problems.
- Two times greater risk of infant mortality.
- More likely to go to prison.
- More likely to commit crime.
- Seven times more likely to become pregnant as a teen.
- More likely to face abuse and neglect
- More likely to abuse drugs and alcohol.
- Two times more likely to suffer obesity.
- Two times more likely to drop out of high school.[7]
- More than twice as likely to commit suicide.[8]

Shockingly, children from fatherless homes are 279 percent
more likely to carry guns and deal drugs than peers living with their
fathers.[9] Indeed the majority of the deadliest mass shootings in the
United States have been perpetrated by men not raised by their
fathers.[10] In a nutshell, boys without fathers tend toward violence,
and girls tend toward risky sexual behavior and personally destructive
relationships with men. Simply put, scholars agree that "changing
family structure is the greatest long term threat to U.S. children."[11]
The prevailing cultural narrative in America today is that it is not
necessarily best (or even better) for kids to grow up in a family with
a married father and mother, but the statistics don't lie.

---

[7]   Ibid.
[8]   http://fathers.com/statistics-and-research/the-consequences-of-fatherlessness/
[9]   https://fatherhoodfactor.com/us-fatherless-statistics/
[10] https://www.patheos.com/blogs/markmeckler/2018/02/27-deadliest-mass-
      shooters-26-one-thing-common/
[11] Blankenhorn, David. *Fatherless America*, 43.

Godly Dads Matter

We find a much different picture when we look at fathers who love and follow God. Sociologist W. Bradford Wilcox, director of the National Marriage Project, has conducted extensive research on the effects married Christian men have on their wives and children. Wilcox's research reached this conclusion: "conservative Protestant married men with children are consistently the most active and expressive fathers and the most emotionally engaged husbands."[12] In addition, "the coupling between ideology and practice is closest among conservative Protestant family men who attend church regularly."[13] What this means is that Christian men who spend more time in God's house (church) become the best husbands and dads in their own homes. These men don't just say they love their wives and kids; they put their love into action.

No matter what the enemy says or what he has deceived culture into believing, the truth is that God's ways are not only timeless but timely. God's ways still work the best, and they always will. We need godly dads to lead our families. We need godly dads who are tough *for* their wives and children yet tender *with* their wives and children. We need godly dads who show us how to live for God rather than getting caught up in the winds of culture. We need godly dads who show us what God the Father is like and how He feels about us.

In each of the following chapters, we'll explore a common way that dads can distort our view of God the Father and the effects this has on our lives, then we'll move on to explore what the Bible says about who the Father is and how He feels about us. Each chapter ends with a prayer rather than reflection questions. I don't want you to talk to yourself (most women are already quite good at that!). I want you to talk to your Father. Feel free to pray the prayer as written if you can't seem to find your own words. Or simply use it as inspiration to express what you are thinking and feeling. Praying like this felt awkward for me at first too, but I have learned to talk to God like He's my Dad. I want that for you too. Let's get started.

---

[12] Wilcox, W. Bradford. *Soft Patriarchs, New Men*, 195.
[13] Ibid.

2

My Heavenly Father Is Always with Me

My dad abandoned me.

One of my favorite old hymns says, "This is my Father's world. He shines in all that's fair. In the rustling grass, I hear him pass. He speaks to me everywhere." God is indeed everywhere, as mysterious as that concept is to our human minds. Theologians call this God's omnipresence. The reason I love the words of this hymn is that it reminds us that God's everywhere presence isn't as an impersonal force but rather a personal Father. He speaks to us in sunrises, cool breezes on a hot day, in a delicious meal, a conversation with a friend, the laughs of our kids, and so on. God is a Father who wants to speak to and be near his kids. In his book *God Is Closer than You Think*, John Ortberg says, "The story of the Bible isn't primarily about the desire of people to be with God; it's the desire of God to be with people."[14] God made you because He loves you and wants a relationship with you. He wants to be near you. And because He loves you, He cares about every aspect of your life—your physical, emotional, mental, spiritual, and relational health.

---

[14] Ortberg, John, *God Is Closer Than You Think. 13.*

Dad's Presence Reflects the Father's Presence

God's design for dads is that they'll impart this aspect of His character to their kids. As dads involve themselves in the lives of their kids—both the small details and the big deals—children will learn that God the Father is like this too. Joseph was this kind of a dad to the little boy Jesus.

In coming to earth as a baby, Jesus retained His divine nature, yet he added to it his humanity.[15] Just as all kids have to learn, grow, and mature, so did the boy Jesus. Luke 2:40 says, "And the child grew and became strong, filled with wisdom. And the favor of God was upon him." Jesus started his life on earth as a baby, then became a child, then a young man, then a mature man. He needed the tender love of His mom, Mary, but he also needed the guidance of His earthly dad, Joseph, to help Him mature, just like regular people do. The Bible doesn't tell us many details about Joseph, but that doesn't mean his relationship with Jesus wasn't significant. In his book *Our Heavenly Father*, Robert Frost explains that Joseph was chosen by God to be Jesus's earthly dad "because he was a man of faith, obedience, loyalty, and above all, a man of humility and love."[16] Indeed the angel of the Lord appeared to him in a dream three times, and all three times Joseph did exactly as the Lord had said.[17]

Before Jesus went into full-time ministry around the age of thirty, He was a carpenter with His dad, Joseph. As such, He would have spent years learning how to select the proper materials and tools for each task. He probably hit His thumb or cut Himself from time to time. He learned how to make a plan and see a project through from beginning to end. While women can easily build relationships by sitting and talking with one another, men tend to bond while they do things, whether it's throwing a football, grilling in the backyard, or watching the game on TV. So imagine the conversations that happened between Joseph and Jesus as they worked in their shop.

---

[15] See Hebrews 2:14–18.
[16] Frost, Robert, *Our Heavenly Father*, 27.
[17] See Matthew 1:20, 2:13 and 19.

Perhaps they talked about how nature reflects God's glory and majesty. Or maybe they discussed that as they were crafting wood into something beautiful, so, too, did God craft the earth and everything in it. Perhaps they discussed the discipline and perseverance required to become a master carpenter. Maybe they had tough or deceitful customers, and they discussed how to be discerning of people. Joseph was young Jesus's first introduction into how to interact with the world around Him. All dads are supposed to model Joseph in this way. They are to lead, guide, and help their kids grow in maturity so they are ready to hit the ground running when it's their time to head out into the world as adults. And in all of that, they are showing their children that God is a Father who loves, leads, and guides them every day of their lives. Robert Frost sums up the effect of the relationship between Joseph and Jesus:

> Through Joseph's life, little Jesus learned about the Fatherhood of God. There came a time in the young manhood of Jesus when His dependency upon Joseph as a father-figure was totally transferred to His heavenly Father. A communion with God was established which no longer required the intermediary of an earthly father.[18]

Jesus and Joseph's relationship embodies Proverbs 22:6 which says, "Train up a child in the way he should go; and even when he is old he will not depart from it." If you are a parent, you know what it's like to yearn for the day when your child has their own relationship with God. They don't cease to need you as a parent, but their primary reliance is on God and His presence in their life. Our relationship with our dad can greatly contribute to sending us on the right path, not only in life but also in relationship with God the Father.

---

[18] Frost, Robert. *Our Heavenly Father,* 30.

When Dad Leaves

Though we don't know exactly what happened to Joseph, we do know that he was not recorded in the Bible as being present for any of Jesus's ministry activities. For example, Mary was at the wedding at Cana where Jesus performed his first miracle of turning water into wine, but the Bible does not mention Joseph. Neither did experience the culmination of Jesus's ministry—His death on the cross and resurrection from the dead. As Jesus was dying, He called down to his best friend John and asked Him to care for Mary. The likely conclusion to draw is that Joseph had already died. Perhaps your dad died when you were a child. Perhaps your dad is facing a terminal illness and you don't know if he will continue to live or for how long. Or maybe your dad is aging and you know there will soon come a day when he will die. Losing a father to death is tragic, and it seems that Jesus knew something of what this was like.

On the show *Parenthood*, I remember so clearly the episode in which Zeek Braverman, the family patriarch, died (My apologies to any of you who haven't seen the show. It's still worth watching.) I dearly loved his character over the course of the entire series because he showed so much of what a dad should be—tough *for* his family, tender *with* his family, loving and faithful. He wasn't a perfect dad or grandpa, but he dearly loved his family and was always there for them. I will admit that I cried when Zeek's character died. I know he wasn't a real person, but he gave me a picture of what fatherhood is, and I felt sad to see it end.

"Historically, the principal cause of fatherlessness was paternal death... Today the principal cause of fatherlessness is paternal choice," explains David Blankenhorn in his book *Fatherless America*. Today 40 percent of children are born out of wedlock, and nearly 25 percent of kids live in a home without a dad. These kids are much less likely to have a close relationship with their dad and experience his influence in their daily lives. Some of them don't even know who their dad is. Dads are out there, but for one reason or another, they do not live with their children. Blankenhorn explains why this "volitional fatherlessness" is so detrimental:

> Though paternal death and paternal abandonment are frequently treated as sociological equivalents, these two phenomena could hardly be more different in their impact upon children and upon the larger society. To put it simply, death puts an end to fathers. Abandonment puts an end to fatherhood... When a father dies, a child grieves. [I have lost someone I love.] When a father leaves, a child feels anxiety and self-blame. [What did I do wrong? Why doesn't my father love me?] Death is final. [He won't come back.] Abandonment is indeterminate. [What would make him come back?][19]

Blankenhorn explains that when a dad dies, the child's memory of Dad lives on: "In this sense, the child is still fathered."[20] However when a dad chooses to leave, the child's very idea of fatherhood leaves with him. This child is essentially "unfathered."[21] If you can identify with this, I am sorry. Being abandoned by your dad causes pain to the depths of your soul. Sadly, this is quite common. "For the first time in our nation's history, millions of men are today voluntarily abdicating their fatherhood."[22] Today, millions of children are not only losing their dads but also losing the idea of fatherhood; they don't know what a dad is supposed be or do. Two equally tragic outcomes are (1) some children maintain a longing for that dad, and (2) some don't think they need one. Whether you leave the open wound or you try to deny its existence, the pain remains. This loss of the idea of "dad" is then projected onto God the Father: "Is there a God? Does He love me, or is He angry with me? Will He leave me

---

[19] Blankenhorn, David. *Fatherless America*, 23.
[20] Ibid. 24
[21] Ibid. 24
[22] Blankenhorn, David. *Fatherless America*, 23.

like my dad left me?" The negative impact of volitional fatherlessness truly cannot be overstated. It is devastating both to individuals and to society as a whole.

The Father's Promise

As we look at God's Word, we see who He is. We see that He most definitely is not a Father who will leave us. In fact, the most frequent promise God makes in the Bible is 'I will be with you.' We can infer that this is perhaps a tender spot for people, so God graciously repeats Himself throughout Scripture. In his book *God is Closer Than You Think*, John Ortberg explains, "Before Adam and Eve ever sinned or needed forgiveness, they were promised God's presence. He would walk with them in the cool of the day... The unity of the Bible is discovered in the development of life with-God as a reality on earth centered in the person of Jesus."[23] The whole point of God creating us, sending Jesus to rescue us, and sustaining us until we are with Him in heaven is that He is a Father who wants to be with His kids. God your Father wants to dwell with you, and He has promised to never, ever leave you. He is there for all of life's big moments and all of the small ones in-between. He is always with you

when you graduate from college or get a promotion at work,
when you get married,
when your divorce is finalized,
when you buy your first house,
when you have a difficult conversation with someone,
when your child throws a tantrum in the grocery store,
when you are in the car, paying bills, or waiting at the dentist,
when you get a phone call with tragic news,
when you are _____.

---

[23] Frost, Robert, *Our Heavenly Father*, 15.

You fill in the blank. Where in your life would it help you to realize that your loving Father is present with you? Where in your life have you forgotten to look for Him? If you grew up with a dad who left you, or if you had a good dad but still struggle to rely on God more than yourself, know that your heavenly Father promises that He will never leave you. His desire is to be with you always.

Whatever happens in your life—or even this day or this hour—God is with you. He wants His presence to make you feel safe, loved, and at peace.

Practical Tips for Experiencing God's Presence

Have you ever heard someone say (or maybe even said yourself), "I don't know what to do in this situation, but I really need God to show up." But as we've seen, God is everywhere all the time. He's watching over us; He goes before us; and His presence with us never wavers or diminishes. So it's safe to assume that if we don't feel God's presence, it's not Him that needs to "show up." It's us. If God is always paying attention to us and present with us, the reason we might not feel His presence is that *we* are not paying attention to *Him*. That might be tough to swallow, but it's true.

I'll be honest, this was a tough section for me to write. Lately I've spent a lot more time trying to get things done than I have being with God. I've been snappish with people; I've had a tense feeling in my chest (Hello, stress!). I haven't been sleeping well, and I've been struggling to relax. There isn't anything catastrophic going on in my life, but rather there are countless little things that are adding up to feel like a lot. I felt God urging me to press pause on writing this chapter and to live it first. I needed to spend time with Him. I didn't hide from the world or go off the grid. I still had responsibilities to take care of. But I did cut out the fluff in my life to make more room for me to spend with my Father. Here are ten practices I've adopted to help me learn to feel God's presence no matter what my day brings:[24]

1. *Recognize God is present.* It sounds so obvious, but waking up and first talking to God orients my mind and connects my soul to Him before anything else is allowed to hijack my attention. I pray that God would help me to remember that He's with me and ask Him to show me throughout the day how I can love and serve the people in my life. As the day progresses, I also take time to pause and reconnect with Him. Practically speaking, this often takes place in the car when I'm driving to pick up my kids at school since it's usually the only time I sit still all day. I take the ten-minute drive to school to praise God for the ways that He's been present with me helped me that day, and I ask Him to give me peace and energy I need to finish the day strong.

2. *Continually talk to God.* Before venting to others about my frustrations or seeking their advice to my struggles, I talk to God. Instead of allowing my thoughts to snowball, I also talk to God. I talk to him in simple, frank language. I speak to him like a little kid would talk to their daddy or how I would chat with a close friend. No, I don't do this perfectly. Yes, I still talk to trusted friends. But I keep practicing talking to God *first*. This is what the apostle Paul means in 1 Thessalonians 5:17 when he says we should "pray without ceasing."

3. *Detach from my phone.* My phone is usually within arm's reach of my body. I can't even count how many times a day I check in with something on my phone—texts, email, news, Amazon. And I realized I *do* know what it's like to have something be a constant presence in my life—my phone! So in order to connect more with God, I have to

---

[24] A good book on learning to feel God's presence is *The Practice of the Presence of God* by Brother Lawrence. It's a short little book full of helpful insights. These seven tips are my own but are inspired by this book.

disconnect from my phone. For God to be the constant presence in my life, my phone needs to not occupy that spot. So I turn on "do not disturb" and check it only a few times a day or answer it if someone calls. God is a far, far better constant companion than my phone.

4. *Guard my soul.* This is the same idea as detaching from my phone but expanded to other areas of life. Basically I have eliminated anything unnecessary in my life that competes for His presence in my life. For example, I know from many years of experience that one area in which I'm weak is comparing myself to other women. As a result, I do not read about celebrities, fashion, or trends online or in magazines. I do not own a scale and do not know how much I weigh. I limit my own screen time just as I do for my kids. Yes, I'm a pretty intense person, but the goal of all of this is that I want to be present with my Father, my family, and my friends more than anything else. (I am in no way saying that the things I have chosen to limit in my life are things that you have to as well. This is what the Holy Spirit has led me to do in my own life.) I only have a certain amount of time and energy each day, and I want to use it for people and things that truly matter to me.

5. *Surrender completely.* When I see the futility of trying to figure something out on my own, I surrender to God as my Father who wants what is best for me. When I am frustrated with a situation I cannot change, I surrender to Him. When I am weary of bearing the weight of responsibilities on my own, I surrender to Him. Surrendering completely to God and what He has planned is something that I have to decide over and over again. I often tell my kids, "God loves you, He made you, He made the world, and so He knows how life works best," and I have to remind myself of these truths as well. I really do believe His ways are better than mine, even when I don't understand His.

6. *Mundane = Meaningful.* I often hear women say their lives are mundane. Wake up, take care of kids, clean house, run

errands, go to work, and repeat. Do you know who lived most of his life doing mundane things? Jesus. He was a carpenter for nearly 90 percent of his life. The so-called mundane things in life are not a waste of time like we sometimes believe. They are times, like any other, that God is with us. That doesn't make them mundane but miraculous! It is often during my mundane housework that I am able to talk to God. Folding laundry doesn't take many brain cells, which means my mind is free to talk to my Father. Truth be told, most of my writing ideas come to me when I'm sweeping the floor. There's something about the rhythmic motion that quiets my mind. The mundane tasks are also the ones that often communicate to others how much we love them, and by extension, how much God loves them. Just as Jesus washed his disciples' feet, we can show others God's love through doing the jobs that no one else is willing to do.

7. *Return to God quickly.* I still sin. I still try to do things in my own power and forget that God is with me. I still fail my husband and kids. I still feel anxious and stressed. But I also make a practice of turning back to God quickly. Whether I need to confess sin, ask for grace, or gain wisdom, I keep trying to return to God quickly. And He is always there waiting for me.

You might be thinking that this looks like an awful lot of work. Yes, this will take intention and planning on your part, but you can learn to feel God's constant presence in your daily life. Experiencing God in our lives is not just reserved for spiritual moments at church on Sunday or doing morning devotions. Life is practical, so learning to experience God's presence is practical too. As with any other relationship, our relationship with God grows when we invest in it. We need to spend time conversing with Him in prayer. We need to spend time listening to Him in His Word. We need to spend time face-to-face, so to speak, with our Father. That's how relationships grow. And

I can attest that whenever you invest in your relationship with God, you will reap immeasurable benefits.

I practiced these seven tips for several days before I began to realize the effects they were having in my life and my soul; I still had just as much on my plate as before, but my soul didn't feel so harried or anxious. My relationships were more enjoyable because I was more enjoyable to be around! My home was more peaceful because I was experiencing the peace of God in my soul and extending His love and tenderness to my husband and children. Feeling God's constant presence in your life is absolutely worth the effort it takes to learn how.

These seven principles will look differently in your life than they do in mine. (Except for principle number 3; we all would do well to spend less time on our phones!) My goal is to give you some examples and inspire your thinking. In order to determine ways that you can practice experiencing God's constant presence, you need to first talk to Him. If you pray and ask the Holy Spirit to show you specific changes you can make in your life so that you can learn to live in God's constant presence, I am confident that He will answer your prayer. Jeremiah 29:13 declares, "You will seek me and find me, when you seek me with all your heart." That is a promise that you can count on. Remember, God is a Father who wants to be with His kids, and that includes you. You can trust him. You can let your guard down. He will never, ever leave you.

Heavenly Father,
Thank you that you desire to be with me
and that you promise to never leave me.
Thank you that you watch over me
and go before me every moment of every day.
I want to learn to feel your presence
in both the small and big moments in my life.
In Jesus's name,
amen.

3

My Heavenly Father Will Never Forsake Me

My dad emotionally abandoned me.

"I am a daughter of the King." This saying appears on everything nowadays from women's social media profiles to bumper stickers to cute signs that hang on the wall. Whenever I see or hear a woman say this, I can't help but wonder if she had an emotionally distant dad. Let me illustrate what I'm talking about with a story from a woman I know.

Until a few years ago, Lisa had a hard time relating to God as her Father. She didn't have a healthy frame of reference for a father-daughter relationship. At times she felt indifference from her dad and at other times outright rejection. So God as a Father was not something she understood. God as a king? Sure, that was much easier. A king is sovereign and in control of all that is in his dominion. A good king will look out for his people's interests, protecting them and giving them the opportunity to have a fruitful life. However, a king does not have personal relationships with his people nor is he involved with the details of their everyday lives. A common individual getting a personal meeting with a king was incredibly rare. Even Queen Esther was breaking protocol by approaching her husband, King Xerxes, without him summoning her first.[25]

---

[25] Esther 4:11.

Back to Lisa's story. She could understand God as a king. But God as a loving, involved Father who provides for, protects, listens to, comforts, and guides her? No. She had no experience in her life that helped her understand God as a Father like that. In fact, Lisa's experience was the opposite. To her, a father was much more like a distant king. Lisa's dad went to work to put food on the table and a roof over her head. He would hand down consequences when she disobeyed or rebelled. But that was about it. He was more interested in his own work and hobbies than in spending time with her and building their relationship. Though Lisa's dad was physically present, he was emotionally distant.

Viewing God as a king, as Lisa did, is not incorrect; but it is incomplete. God is indeed sovereign and in control over all things, all times, and all peoples. Yet Jesus says He came to reveal the Father to us and to do the Father's will, which was to sacrifice Himself in our place for our sin. Jesus taught us to pray to "our Father," not "our King." Jesus also came to show us the Father's heart and what a relationship as his child looks like.

Consider this. When a police officer is on duty, he wears his uniform, badge, and weapon. He carries out his duty to protect his community and arrests those who break the law. But when he comes home, he doesn't continue to operate as Officer So-and-So. He takes off his uniform and puts on normal clothes. Instead of continuing to patrol the premises for right and wrong, he throws a ball in the yard with his kids, sits down for a family dinner, and reads stories at bedtime. This is similar the difference between viewing God primarily as your King or primarily as your Father. Do you view God more as Officer So-and-So or as Dad?

If you have an easier time viewing God as an emotionally distant king instead of a tender, loving, involved Father, this may be due to the fact that you, like Lisa, have an emotionally distant dad. Issues are sure to arise in relationships—misunderstandings, disagreements, even sinning against one another. But when these issues are allowed to become more important than the relationship itself, the issues push the relationship apart. Another reason your dad may be distant is that he didn't have a good example of a loving father either.

Some dads do the best they can with their daughters, but they just don't know how to be emotionally involved and healthy because they didn't grow up in that kind of environment themselves. Nonetheless this can still have a negative impact on a daughter's view of God.

When someone says they love us but then pulls away emotionally or rejects us altogether, it feels as if they've turned their back on us. The Bible has a word for this feeling of having someone turn their back on you—forsaken. When we have been forsaken by our dads, the enemy seizes on this opportunity to tell us the lie that our Heavenly Father will do the same. Nothing could be further from the truth.

In his *21 Day Inner Healing Journey*, Pastor Jimmy Evans explains, "God eternally promises us two things. The first is that He will never physically leave us. The second is that He will never emotionally forsake us, which means He will never turn His heart away from us."[26] Furthermore, "Regardless of the circumstances or how He feels, God will never change His mind or break His promise. He will NEVER, NEVER, NEVER leave or forsake you. For the rest of eternity your loving Heavenly Father will be with you and His heart will be set on you. You cannot change that—it is an eternally settled fact."[27] God is not a Father who leaves, abandons, or emotionally pulls away from you. He is not a Father who lets issues weaken or break your relationship with Him. Your sin, weaknesses, failures, doubts, struggles, and temptations do not jeopardize how your Father feels about you. He will not forsake you. It is absolutely not who He is.

Jesus Was Forsaken so You Won't Be

Christians often talk about the good news of the Gospel—that Jesus died to save us from the penalty for our sin. In doing so, Jesus was also forsaken by the Father so that we never will be. Let's take a look at the details and events of Jesus's death in our place and pay special attention to this issue of being forsaken.

---

[26] Evans, Jimmy, *21 Day Inner Healing Journey*, 15.
[27] Ibid.

The night before Jesus would die on the cross, He began the evening by eating the last supper with his disciples. He served them by washing their feet and explaining what lay ahead for him, preparing them for what was to come in the next few days. He then retreated to the garden of Gethsemane with Peter, James, and John— his inner circle, so to speak—and asked them to pray for him. They let him down and fell asleep instead. Meanwhile, Jesus "began to be sorrowful and troubled"[28] to the point that he was literally sweating drops of blood.[29] Three times he prayed, "My Father, if it be possible, let this cup pass from me."[30] Jesus knew what He was about to do and that taking the sin of the world upon himself would cause a fracture in His perfect, unbroken relationship with the Father. Yet He prayed, "Nevertheless, not as I will, but as you will." He also knew that though the pain of this broken relationship would be excruciating, his pain was for a purpose. The Father, motivated by his overflowing love for you and for me, sent Jesus to take away the sin that separated us from Him. He is not a Father who lets anything stand in the way of His relationship with his kids.

Jesus's spiritual torment in the Garden was made worse by the physical torment He endured after His arrest. He spent the rest of the night enduring false trials and beatings that left Him unrecognizable.[31] His body was shredded and in agony. Many men who suffered the same fate as Jesus died from the beatings alone. Jesus was then forced to carry his own wooden cross up the hill to his

---

[28] Matthew 26:37

[29] Luke 22:44

[30] Matthew 26:39, 42, 44

[31] Isaiah 52:14. Jesus was beaten with a flagellum. According to the International Standard Bible Dictionary, a flagellum was "A Roman implement for severe bodily punishment... It consisted of a handle to which several cords or leather thongs were affixed, which were weighted with jagged pieces of bone or metal to make the blow more painful and effective... The victim was tied to a post (Acts 22:25), and the blows were applied to the back and loins, sometimes even, in the wanton cruelty of the executioner, to the face and the bowels. In the tense position of the body, the effect can easily be imagined. So hideous was the punishment that the victim usually fainted and not rarely died under it." (https://www.blueletterbible.org/search/Dictionary/viewTopic.cfm?topic=IT0007712)

crucifixion site. Depending on whether Jesus carried the entire cross or just the horizontal crossbar, scholars believe He would have had to carry between one hundred and three hundred pounds. Splinters of wood no doubt bored into the open flesh on his shredded back. Though Jesus was young and strong, He had been beaten so badly that He couldn't make it the whole way up the hill on his own. A man named Simon of Cyrene helped carry Jesus's cross the rest of the way. Finally, they arrived at the place of crucifixion. And Jesus's hands, which had once driven nails through pieces of wood, were now themselves nailed down.

Jesus was crucified at nine o'clock in the morning and hung on the cross for hours.[32] At noon, while the blazing sun was straight overhead, the sky went pitch-black.[33] It was as if creation itself anticipated what was about to happen. A few hours later, Jesus cried out, "My God, my God, why have you forsaken me?"[34] There's that word, *forsaken*. Yes, Jesus's death paid the penalty for our sin that separated us from God. Yes, Jesus's death in our place means we get his record of perfect obedience and righteousness. His death also means that He was forsaken instead of us. The song "How Deep the Father's Love" beautifully illustrates this:

> How deep the Father's love for us
> How vast beyond all measure
> That He should give His only Son
> To make a wretch His treasure
>
> How great the pain of searing loss
> The Father turns His face away
> As wounds which mar the Chosen One
> Bring many sons to glory

---

[32] Mark 15:25
[33] Mark 15:33–34
[34] Matthew 27:46

Behold the man upon a cross
My sin upon His shoulders
Ashamed, I hear my mocking voice
Call out among the scoffers

It was my sin that held Him there
Until it was accomplished
His dying breath has brought me life
I know that it is finished

I will not boast in anything
No gifts, no power, no wisdom
But I will boast in Jesus Christ
His death and resurrection

Why should I gain from His reward?
I cannot give an answer
But this I know with all my heart
His wounds have paid my ransom

On the cross, the Father turned his face away from His Son, breaking their perfect eternal union, if ever so briefly. When Jesus finally breathed his last, "the earth shook, and the rocks were split."[35] So cataclysmic was the break in the perfect relationship between God the Father and God the Son that creation couldn't remain at peace. In that moment, God punished Jesus for sin—yours, mine, everyone's. Your relationship with the Father is so important to Him that He took it upon Himself to remove the barrier of sin between the two of you by placing it on His Son instead. There is no punishment left for you. You have no outstanding debt with the Father. Jesus took care of it. It is finished. The Father turned his back on Jesus so that He'll never have to turn his back on you.

The promise that God gave to Joshua before he began to lead Israel into the promised land is the same promise He gives us today:

---

[35] Matthew 27:51.

"I will not leave you or forsake you… Do not be frightened, and do not be dismayed, for the LORD your God is with you wherever you go."[36] Your dad may have allowed issues to get in the way of your relationship. He may have emotionally pulled away from you, rejected you, or forsaken you. If that describes your experience, I truly am sorry. Thankfully, God's love is greater than your dad's rejection. Psalm 27:10 says, "Though my father and mother forsake me, the LORD will receive me." Your Heavenly Father has promised that He will never leave you or forsake you, and you don't need to be afraid that He will.

Learning this was life-changing for Lisa. That sounds like an overstatement, but it's not. Lisa felt that she finally had a name for how she had felt for so long. Lisa felt forsaken by her dad, and as a result, she did not believe that God would want to be in a close relationship with her. Lisa didn't believe that God wanted to be involved in the details of her daily life or that God loved her enough to be her Father. This affected her marriage and parenting too. Lisa never felt afraid that her husband would leave, but she just assumed a certain level of emotional distance would always be present in their marriage. With her children, Lisa was emotionally disconnected as well. When they sinned, she wanted them to feel the weight of that. She cared more about proving them wrong and herself right than about staying connected to them in a relationship. When they struggled with the same things over and over, Lisa didn't draw closer to them in compassion. She actually drew away in frustration. Until Lisa understood that the Father sent His own Son to be forsaken in her place and that He would never forsake her, she didn't know how to be close to anyone else. Lisa was operating as the daughter of a distant king, not the daughter of a tender Father. Once Lisa understood that God would never forsake her, she was able to receive His love and extend it to others as well.

At this point, some of you might be thinking, "Okay wait a minute. But God *is* a king. He wants us to spread the Good News of salvation through Jesus. He wants us to love and serve people. He

---

[36] Joshua 1:5, 9.

wants us to teach our kids to know Him." Yes, all of those statements are true. However, God cares more about you as His daughter than about what you can do for Him and His kingdom. Yes, He's got good things for us to do, but He isn't primarily a king who gives you a mission. He's a Father who invites you to go to work with Him.

His Face Is Toward You

In Numbers 6:24–26, God instructs the priests to bless the people of Israel: "The Lord bless you and keep you; the Lord make his face to shine upon you and be gracious to you; the Lord lift up his countenance upon you and give you peace."[37] This is one of my favorite scriptures; it reminds me that God's face is not turned away from me but is always toward me. Think about your relationships with others. How do you know that other people care about you? Are they listening to you? Are they interested in you? Do they look you in the eye? We live in an age where we're all distracted by various screens and technology. Most people don't read books or write letters anymore. We read articles and social media posts in little snippets. Even most of our conversation occurs at a distance over text, email, or social media posts. What a rare thing it is to have someone give you their eyes for any length of time. But the Lord's face is set toward you, and His eyes are on you. In fact, I now pray those verses from Numbers as a blessing over my daughters every day when I drop them off at school. I want them to know from the time that they're little girls that God the Father's face is toward them every minute of their day and that it always will be.

The Holy Spirit transformed this truth I knew in my head into one I felt deep in my heart one day as we were leaving church. Our kids were very little at that time. My husband is a pastor at our church, so he was going to stay all day, and I was heading home to give the little ones a nap. Getting four little kids into car seats is like herding squirrels, so he had come out to the parking lot to help me when we ran into an older pastor at the church. This man oozes

---

[37] Numbers 6:24–26

fatherliness. He's in his seventies, is tall, strong, and tough but at the same time so tender and wise. He asked us how we were doing, as we'd recently had our fourth baby. And I'm sure, with a tired smile, I said something like, "We're doing okay." I will never forget how he looked at me—a huge smile, full eye contact, and a face full of kindness. Then he gently put his hand on the back of my head and said, "Bless you." It was as if, through this man's tender touch, God communicated to me, "This is what kind of Father I am."

Tears instantly welled up in my eyes as the pastor walked away into the church. My husband turned around, saw me crying, and exclaimed, "What happened?" I explained that I had never in my life experienced fatherly love like that.

"So this is a good thing?" he asked.

Oh yes, a very good thing. My tears weren't sad tears. They were healing tears, grateful tears! Jesus's work on the cross removes any distance that existed between you and the Father, so He will forever be faced toward you and looking at you with a warm, kind, delighted face full of love. And what's even better, He also happens to be the King.

Heavenly Father,
Thank you that you will never forsake me
and that your face is always toward me in love.
Thank you for sending Jesus to take my place on the cross
so that I never have to experience distance from You.
Father, I pray that your Spirit would remind me
that your face is forever toward me in love.
In Jesus's Name,
Amen.

4

My Heavenly Father Knows
Me and Loves Me

My dad didn't truly know me.

There's a saying "a true friend is someone who knows your faults and loves you anyway." It's what we all want. When someone knows your strengths, weaknesses, dreams, and fears and still loves you, that creates security both in your heart and in the relationship. A dad is in a unique position to instill this secure love in his daughter from a young age. As the head of the family, a dad is the one who creates a sense of stability and security in the home. The result is that home is a place where a daughter is loved and accepted no matter what. Even when she sins and makes mistakes, this loving environment allows her to gain confidence and security that carries into the rest of her life. When a dad loves his daughter for who she is, flaws, quirks and all, she learns something of what God the Father's love is like—strong, secure, unchanging.

Unfortunately, this is not the experience that many women grow up with. One of these women was Amanda. Amanda's relationship with her dad was superficial. She can't recall sharing her thoughts, feelings, or dreams with him. She can't remember ever having a face-to-face conversation where she was allowed to ask questions about life, growing up, or the world around her. The result was that she kept all her questions and uncertainties inside. For the most part, Amanda received attention and notice from her dad when she did well in school or sports. Amanda reasoned, "If my own dad doesn't even care to know what was in my heart, why would anyone else?" This contributed to her being painfully shy in school. Amanda would never raise her hand in class even though she almost always knew the answers. She loathed working on group projects and would feel incredibly anxious if she had to give a presentation in front of the class. Amanda was terrified that if she messed up, people's opinions of her would be forever changed. Despite this fear, Amanda's desire to have people really know her, all of her, never changed. She lived many years of her life in this conflict between wanting to be known by others but hiding from them at the same time.

When we don't grow up with a secure sense of being loved for who we are, we often try to find an external way to measure if we are worthy of being loved and accepted. For women, this is often in the form of comparison. Yep, we're going there, but I'll go first so, hopefully you'll feel more comfortable. Several years ago, I was in a Bible study with a handful of other women from our church. I had just gotten married, but most of these women had been married for some time and had children already. I felt like they were "real women," and I was just starting out as a "grown up" even though we were all the same age. I also thought they were super stylish; they were amazing cooks (I felt nervous every week when deciding what to contribute to our weekly dinner); and their homes were decorated in that perfectly effortless, comfortable but totally curated way. All of these things were a point of comparison between them and me, and I always felt lacking. I felt unworthy to be in their group, like I was just faking it. My appearance wasn't as stylish; my cooking skills were subpar; and I lived in a newlywed basement apartment. Strikes one, two, and three. I felt as if I didn't measure up to these women like they were completely out of my league. And so instead of building friendships with them, feeling connected to them, and loved by them, I turned them into my competition. Is this ringing any bells? Please tell me I'm not alone here.

This comparison also stretched into how I felt about my physical appearance. Everywhere I went—even church—I would notice the woman who just had a baby but was back into normal jeans. I would notice the woman who seemed to have put on a little weight or chopped off her hair, always sizing up my comparative beauty next to hers. Am I beautiful enough? Am I in good enough physical shape? Am I dressed well? And what those superficial questions are really asking are, "Am I enough? Am I too much? Am I acceptable? Am I lovable?" When I thought I looked better than one woman, I would feel more secure and lovable. Until I saw another woman whom I thought looked better than me, and then I'd feel unworthy and unlovable. It was a roller coaster of inner dialogue in my mind all day, every day.

Now I'm going to take a detour for a minute, but stick with me because it's important. We take the topic of "body image" as a given in our lives. However, in the history of the world, body image is a fairly recent concept, a term that was first coined in the 1930s. Body image refers to a person's *subjective perception* of their own physical appearance, usually in relation to how others see them or some cultural ideal. "Body image" is essentially how I feel I measure up to the images I see in the culture, media, and people around me. God did not create "body image"; people did. And we are consumed by it. Never before in the history of the world have people been so continuously and forcefully bombarded with images of a cultural ideal of beauty. Social media, selfies, photo filters—we know that what we see online and in magazines is largely smoke and mirrors, but we are still deeply affected by what we see. The stream of images and information tempts us to pursue culture's standards of beauty, and we have been naïve about how much of this temptation we can handle. When our personal media consumption goes unchecked, preoccupation with body image is sure to follow. I believe body image is a lie from Satan. It's the lie that says, "You'll be worthy of love and acceptance if you are _____." Except what goes in that blank is always changing.

I am not saying we all need to get off the Internet or go back to flip phones that only call and text. But I am suggesting that we use discernment and ask ourselves if anything needs to change in our media consumption. Culture's line of what is acceptable, preferable, and praiseworthy is always moving, which means that when we gauge how well we are loved, liked, and valued by culture's standards, we are chasing a moving target. What an exhausting and discouraging cycle. This is not what our loving Father intends for His daughters.

You know the saying, "God loves you just the way you are but too much to leave you that way?" It's true. The Father doesn't base His love for you on what you look like, what you achieve in school or the workplace, how many children you have or don't have, how smart you are, how much you struggle with temptation or sin. He doesn't even love you for how often you read your Bible, serve the church, help others, or do things for His kingdom. No, He loves you because you are His daughter. That's it. Yet because He's your Father, He wants to grow you in the areas you're weak. He wants to cleanse and forgive your sin and send the Holy Spirit to empower you to live a godly life. He wants to heal the pain you carry in your heart from people who have sinned against you.

Colossians 1:15 says that Jesus "is the image of the invisible God." He came to show us what the Father is like. On numerous occasions in the Gospels, Jesus encountered women who were not admired or esteemed by others. There was nothing in the women's outward appearance or achievements that made them acceptable to their communities; they were viewed as outcasts. If they had tried to measure their self-worth based on others' opinions of them, they would have found themselves labeled such things as whore, unclean, and sinful. Yet in his interactions with them, Jesus shows us the Father's heart toward women who have flaws and failures, just like you and me. Let's take a look at some examples that illustrate that "the LORD sees not as man sees: man looks on the outward appearance, but the LORD looks on the heart."[38]

Jesus and the Woman of Samaria (John 4:1–42)

While Jesus was traveling from Judea to Galilee, He passed through Samaria and stopped in a town called Sychar. The Samaritans were a mixed-race group of people, partly of Jewish and partly of

---

[38] 1 Samuel 16:7

Gentile ancestry. Both groups were disdained by Jews and non-Jews alike.[39] The Bible tells us that Jesus was weary from his journey and sat at the town's well. It was noon, which means it was quite hot with the sun directly overhead. Normally women would draw water in the morning when it was still cool, but Jesus ran into a woman drawing water in the heat of the day. This woman, we soon discover, had already gone through five husbands and was currently living with a sixth man. This is the reason she was drawing water after all of the other women had gone home. She was unacceptable to her community—to them she was a woman of ill repute from an inferior race. This woman did not have a good husband nor did she have friends. She must have felt so alone and so unloved. Yet how did Jesus treat to her? With love, tenderness, and an invitation to believe in Him and receive the Holy Spirit, who He said would be a spring of living water in her that would never run dry! The most astonishing thing to me is the woman's response. She went back into town, to the people whom she was previously trying to avoid, and said, "Come see a man who told me all that I ever did. Can this be the Christ?"[40] After hearing this, people came out to see Jesus. He knew everything about her, and that was a good thing! Every unsavory thing in her past that had driven away people in her community did not drive away the One who mattered the most—her Savior. This "immoral" woman became the first evangelist recorded in the Bible, for "many Samaritans from that town believed in him because of the woman's testimony, 'He told me all that I ever did.'"[41] God knows all you've ever done, and He loves you.

Jesus Anointed by a Sinful Woman (Luke 7:36–50)

In Luke 7, Jesus was eating at the house of a Pharisee. Pharisees were strict adherents of the Jewish law and had piled more of their own laws on top of the ones God had given. Apparently, they didn't

---

[39] ESV study Bible note on John 4:4.
[40] John 14:29
[41] John 4:39

believe God had gone far enough, so they arrogantly took "holiness" to a whole new level. Jesus often criticized their hypocrisy, for they were known to look very spiritual and righteous on the outside but weren't very kind or loving on the inside. In this passage from Luke 7, a woman "who was a sinner" came to see Jesus at a Pharisee's house and brought a flask of expensive, fragrant ointment. When she saw Jesus, she began to weep so hard that she wet his feet with her tears. She bent down to wipe Jesus's feet with her hair, kissed them, and anointed them with the ointment. Her heart was so full of love and worship for Jesus that she freely expressed how she felt despite the fact that this would have been very inappropriate in their culture. Simon, the Pharisee, couldn't believe that Jesus was letting a "sinner" touch him. Yet Jesus pointed out how Simon showed him no such hospitality while this woman had not ceased to kiss his feet since she arrived. Jesus said, "Therefore I tell you, her sins, which are many, are forgiven—for she loved much." And to top it all off, Jesus addressed the "sinful woman" directly: "Your sins are forgiven… Your faith has saved you; go in peace."[42] If you belong to Jesus, the same goes for you: your sins are forgiven, go in peace.

Jesus and the Woman with a Blood Disease (Luke 8:43–48)

On another occasion, Jesus was on his way to Jairus's house. This man was a ruler in the synagogue. His daughter was dying, and Jesus was on his way to help. While on the journey, crowds of people surrounded and pressed upon Jesus. In the midst of the commotion, there was a poor woman who had suffered from a blood disease for twelve years. This would have made for a lonely life, for her blood discharge made her unclean and thus cut off from many social and religious relationships.[43] This woman was destitute, for she had spent all her money on doctors and found no relief, no healing. So in an act of faith, she reached out and touched just the hem of Jesus's garment

---

[42] Luke 7:48, 50
[43] ESV Study Bible Note Luke 8:43

as He passed by, "and immediately her discharge of blood ceased."[44] Jesus stopped. "Someone touched me, for I perceive that power has gone out from me."[45] The woman came trembling and fell down at Jesus's feet. She proclaimed to everyone that she had touched Jesus and received immediate healing. "And he said to her, 'Daughter, your faith has made you well; go in peace.'"[46] I love that Jesus called her "daughter." What a depiction of his Father's heart toward this precious woman of faith. Just like the Samaritan woman and the woman at the Pharisee's house, here again is a woman who was unacceptable and probably ignored by her community but loved, forgiven, and brought near by Jesus.

The Woman Caught in Adultery (John 7:53–8:11)

In John's Gospel, there is a story that is not included in the earliest manuscripts of the Bible, but most scholars believe it did truly occur during Jesus's ministry. One morning while Jesus was teaching at the temple in Jerusalem, the scribes and the Pharisees brought to Him a woman whom they accused of being an adulteress. They said they caught her in the act, but where was the man she was with? And how exactly did they catch her in the act? The whole thing is suspicious and cruel. They were clearly using her to test Jesus, pointing out that the Law of Moses requires such women to be stoned. Jesus, in his typical way, did not succumb to the Pharisees's trap but instead replied that anyone in the crowd who was without sin themselves could throw the first stone. One by one, they all went away. Jesus and the woman were left standing alone. Think for a moment how you would feel if you were this woman. Was she terrified that her sin had been exposed to her community, let alone to the one who some say is the Messiah? Was she afraid she would indeed be stoned?

---

44 Luke 8:44
45 Luke 8:46
46 Luke 8:48

Jesus said to her, "Woman, where are they? Has no one condemned you?"[47] She replied, "No one, Lord." And Jesus said, "Neither do I condemn you; go and from now on sin no more."[48] Jesus acknowledged that she had in fact sinned. Yet He showed her compassion rather than condemnation. He does the same for you, for "there is therefore now no condemnation for those who are in Christ Jesus."[49] In Christ, you are not condemned as a sinner but forgiven and loved as a daughter.

Women in Jesus's Family (Matthew 1:1–16)

Jesus's own genealogy in the book of Matthew contains women who were flawed, misunderstood, and yet used by God the Father to bring our Savior into the world. There is Tamar, who tricked her father-in-law into getting her pregnant (Gen. 38). Then we have Rahab, the prostitute who by faith hid and protected two Hebrew spies who came to survey the land of Jericho. "When the city of Jericho fell (6:17–25), Rahab and her whole family were preserved according to the promise of the spies, and were incorporated among the Jewish people. She afterwards became the wife of Salmon, a prince of the tribe of Judah."[50] Rahab also became the mother of Boaz. He later married Ruth, a Moabite widow who was looked down upon by her community as a foreigner and alone in the world. Boaz redeemed her and brought her into the family of God. We'll explore Ruth's story in-depth in another chapter. Next, there is Bathsheba, the wife of Uriah, whose beauty captured the attention of King David. David got her pregnant, then had her husband Uriah killed in battle to cover up his adultery. Bathsheba later became the mother of King Solomon. Finally, there is Mary. A young, unmarried, virgin girl from a very small town who turns up pregnant. She was no doubt seen as

---

[47] Jesus's calling her "woman" was not harsh but actually a tender way to speak in that day. He called his mother Mary "woman" at the wedding in Cana. See John 2:1–12.

[48] John 8:9–11

[49] Romans 8:1

[50] Easton's Bible Dictionary entry for "Rahab"

immoral and unfaithful to her soon-to-be-husband Joseph. All of these women were not acceptable to their communities because of who they were and what they had done, but they were loved by God and part of His plan to bring our Savior into the world.

Just like these women, God the Father sees you—your likes and dislikes, your hopes and fears, your joys and pains—and He loves you. You don't have to be afraid of showing him who you truly are. He already knows everything, and He loves you. You don't have to compare yourself to other women or gauge how acceptable you are to Him based on other people's opinions. His opinion is the only one that truly matters. "The LORD sees not as man sees: man looks on the outward appearance, but the LORD looks on the heart."[51]

Heavenly Father,
Thank you that you see all of me.
Thank you that your love never changes,
whether I do right or I do wrong.
Thank you that you made me unique, and that's a good thing.
I thank you for sending Jesus to show us
that you treat women, including me, with forgiveness,
tenderness, and love.
Father, I ask that your Spirit would
make these truths real in my heart.
In Jesus's Name,
Amen.

---

[51] 1 Samuel 16:7

5

My Heavenly Father Demonstrates His Love for Me

My dad didn't show his love for me

The dad faces his daughter, somewhat awkwardly and shuffling from one foot to the other. They are waiting in the church foyer as he's about to walk her down the aisle and see her marry a kind young man. She looks beautiful and grown-up in her lacy white gown, flowing veil, and bouquet of roses. The dad struggles but finally works up the courage to say, "You know I love you, right?"

And the daughter mutters something like, "Yeah, sure."

This is a picture of a dad who is physically present but emotionally distant from his daughter. Love and affection and warmth have not marked their day-to-day relationship, so an occasional "you know I love you" doesn't mean very much. For those of us who grew up with emotionally distant dads, it is easy to project this emotional distance on to God the Father. As a result, we struggle to enjoy a close, warm, loving relationship with Him.

Now let me say that sometimes dads also grew up in emotionally distant homes so they are unsure of how to express love for their daughters. They wish they know how to have a close relationship, but they just don't. I know several women who grew up with this kind of dad. They always had the things they needed and wanted in life—home, food, toys, vacations, sports. Many dads express their love in this way—by working hard and providing for the family. They think providing for all their daughters' needs and wants is enough and don't realize that while their provision may be very appreciated, daughters also need appropriate, tender, warm affection from their dads such as hugs, kisses on the cheek, snuggles at bedtime, encouraging words when they are anxious, and praying with her.

I can still remember visiting a certain aunt and uncle's house when I was a kid. My aunt and uncle were both huggers. Every time we arrived and every time we packed up to head home, we'd get hugs from both of them and all of their kids. When my uncle hugged me, it was tender, loving, and completely appropriate. I was unused to this fatherly affection, however, so it felt confusing. Part of me felt loved and safe. But another part of me was a bit afraid because it was so foreign to me. To think of that now makes me sad. I wish I could have just enjoyed that display of fatherly love from my uncle.

Affection from a dad is so important for a little girl because it demonstrates love. Think about it—if someone says they love you but never shows you, do you believe that they love you? Love is not truly love unless it's expressed. A father's affection is also crucial for a daughter because it sets the standard for how she believes men should be able to physically interact with her, touch her, and expect affection from her in return. I'm not a psychologist or a counselor, so I can't give you all the possible ways lack of fatherly love can affect a daughter's life, but I can tell you what it looked like in my life, which I think is quite common.

In middle school and high school, the lack of expressed love and affection from my dad made me flat out afraid of boys. I can still remember being in volleyball practice in seventh grade and the boys who had just finished basketball practice in another gym were standing at the doors, watching us. I felt so uncomfortable. But that feeling was ratcheted up when the other girls started telling me that one of the looming boys had a crush on me, and he was an eighth grader. I was terrified. I didn't want boys anywhere near me because I didn't know what would happen. Throughout middle school and high school, this was my posture toward boys. And as a result, I dressed in such a way as to blend in and not draw attention to myself. Other girls would wear cute, feminine (sometimes revealing) outfits, and I tended to wear loose clothing. Socially, I kept to myself as well with my only outing being to youth group on Wednesday nights with one of my girlfriends. I kept my distance from God as well. Though we went church on Sundays, I had zero concept of God being a Father to me or that He wanted a relationship with me. I didn't have any negative or abusive experiences with boys or men; I had no experiences at all. And I was afraid of the unknown.

When I got to college, I'm not sure what changed. Perhaps I just got tired of feeling lonely. But I swung to the opposite side of the pendulum. I ended up dating a guy who had already been to rehab when he was in high school. Clearly I did not know how to be discerning. He marched to the beat of his own drum, didn't care what other people thought about him, and called me a "princess." I liked that he was strong and that he showed me how he felt about me. I spent years on this pendulum, swinging from seeking affection in all the wrong places to feeling guilty and ashamed and hiding in isolation. I ended up feeling exhausted, alone, tainted, and hopeless. When I think of how desperate I was for someone to show me love, I also think about those of you reading who maybe are in that place in your life right now. If you didn't receive appropriate affection from you dad, I am sorry. If you have never before known how deeply God loves you and demonstrates His love for you, I am sorry. I know some of you feel desperate for love, affection, and for someone to prove their love for you. Let me assure you those are good desires. They are God-given desires, ones that He wants to and will fulfill in your heart.

God Tells Us How He Feels About Us

Unlike the dad who says, "You know I love you, right?" God vividly describes in the Bible how He feels toward us as his daughters. As I've said before, we can't explore everything the Bible has to say on this topic in this book. So we'll look at a few examples of God clearly and descriptively expressing how He loves us.

Psalm 17:8 says, "Keep me as the apple of your eye; hide me in the shadow of your wings." In this verse, "apple of your eye" literally means *as the apple, the daughter of the eye*" (Ps. 17:8). The apple of the eye refers to the actual eyeball, with the pupil at the center. "Apple" probably comes from its round shape. Our eyelids automatically close in fierce protection at even the slightest threat of danger to the eye. What this means is that there is nothing in all of creation that is more important to God than his children, which includes you. You are the apple of His eye. In addition, this verse says that God hides us in the shadow of his wings. It's not just mother birds who care for their young. Many father birds help build nests, incubate eggs, bring food for their babies, and stay with their young even after the mother birds have left. I love when God uses his creation to give us a picture of what He is like. Imagine a daddy bird gently protecting, sheltering, and warming his newly hatched, delicate, helpless babies. God is a tender Father like that.

Let's move on to Psalm 18, which was written by King David. In verse 19, we see another word that tells us how God feels about us: "He brought me out into a broad place; he rescued me, because he *delighted* in me" (emphasis mine). David is praising God for delivering him from trouble and danger and instead setting him free because God took pleasure in him. David doesn't say he earned God's rescue or God's pleasure. No, God delighted in David because David was His. Do you know that God also delights in you? You are His daughter, and He takes pleasure in His relationship with you.

In Psalm 103:13, we see that "As a father has compassion to his children, so the LORD shows compassion to those who fear him." The Hebrew word for *compassion* is much richer in meaning. It refers to a soft, cherishing, soothing feeling and to have tender affection toward someone, particularly of parents to children and of the compassion of God toward people. Do you know that God feels tender compassion and affection toward you?

Zephaniah 3:17 is a verse you may be familiar with, but let's try to see it with fresh eyes. It says, "The LORD your God is in your midst, a mighty one who will save; he will rejoice over you with gladness; he will quiet you with his love; he will exult over you with loud singing." God is with you, and He is mighty. You make Him cheerful, full of joy, gladness, and pleasure that overflows into jubilant expression. And while the Father is singing over you, what will you be doing? The phrase that says, "He will quiet you with his love" translates from Hebrew that actually means to be struck deaf and unable to speak. Think about this! God's rejoicing in song over you is so beautiful, so full of love and joy and emotion, that when we experience it, we are overwhelmed by it in the best way possible. It is that kind of display of love that assures us, calms us, and gives us peace. To say that God's love for you is expressive would be a massive understatement.

God Demonstrates His Love

If you've spent any length of time in church, you've probably heard these two verses because of the succinct way they summarize the Gospel:

> For God so loved the world, that he gave his only Son, that whoever believes in him should not perish but have eternal life. (John 3:16 ESV)

> But God shows his love for us in that while we were still sinners, Christ died for us. (Rom. 5:8 ESV)

Usually the preacher, or even us as the reader, places emphasis on certain aspects of these verses. Primarily, that we are sinners who are completely unable to save ourselves. Without the death of Jesus in our place and our belief in Him, we would be condemned to an eternity of suffering apart from God. Emphasis is usually placed on the action: Jesus had to die to save us; we need to believe in Him as Savior. These elements are completely true. But they are not the whole story.

Let's back up to the beginning of these two verses. Who is the first person listed in these verses? Where does all the action start? It starts with God, that is God the Father. In his book *Our Heavenly Father*, Robert Frost says, "By substituting a phrase such as 'our dear heavenly Father' for the word 'God' where appropriate, our personal appreciation of the Father's loving nature is greatly enhanced." So these verses become "For God the Father so loved the world that he gave his only Son…" and "But God the Father shows his love for us…" Do you see how this changes these verses? Jesus came to die to take away the sin that separated us from God because we are completely and utterly unable to achieve that ourselves. But what Jesus did is simply not a transaction (we'll discuss this more in-depth in a later chapter). Jesus lived the perfect life of obedience you and I cannot live, and He died the death in penalty for sin that you and I deserve. This is true. But *why* did He do it? Love. The Father sent His Son Jesus into the world as our Big Brother to rescue us from the plague and penalty of sin so that we could be in eternal, close, intimate relationship of love with our Father. God the Father's love for us was and is so powerful that He was compelled to act and secure our relationship with Him for all time. What a wondrous love indeed!

A Picture of the Father's Love

Though Jesus never married or had children of his own, He demonstrated the Father's heart. Indeed, Colossians 1:15 says that Jesus is the visible image of the invisible God. Jesus clearly demonstrated the Father's love in his interactions with little children. In Luke 18, parents were bringing their small children, even infants, to Jesus so that He could bless them. This was probably a frequent occurrence in Jesus's ministry. In this instance, the disciples scolded the parents for bothering Jesus. I can just picture the disciples, who at that time were still quite "rough around the edges," thinking they were being proactive and protective of their leader. Yet Jesus turned the scolding around onto the disciples! While most ancient cultures at the time regarded children as a burden until they were old enough and strong enough to contribute to the family, Jesus welcomed them tenderly saying, "Let the children come to me."[52] The account of this

---

[52] Mark 10:14, Luke 18:16

story in the Gospel of Mark says that Jesus took the little kids in his arms and blessed them.[53]

Little kids are drawn to people who are warm, fun, and welcoming. Can you picture Jesus scooping up the little girls and kissing them on the forehead? Maybe some of the little boys were hanging on his arms, jumping up on his back, or trying to wrestle him to the ground. Perhaps some of the little girls were rubbing their hands on Jesus's beard like my girls do with their daddy. It seems these children were unaware that they weren't valuable in their culture, but they were very aware that Jesus valued them and loved them. They didn't worry that they didn't have anything to give Jesus. They just ran to his embrace, eager to receive his affection and blessing. Jesus used this as a teaching moment and said that those of us who want to enter the kingdom of God need to have a childlike faith like these little ones did. It's as if Jesus is saying, "Don't worry about what other people say about you. Don't worry about what you've done or that you don't have much to give. Just come to me and receive my love." What a beautiful picture of God the Father's love toward us.

Have you ever seen one of those videos on the Internet of dads who are soldiers returning home to their families after having been deployed overseas? If you haven't, when you're done reading this, I suggest you go look one up and bring some tissues with you. These videos encourage my heart so greatly by giving me a living picture of God the Father's love toward me. These videos show dads and kids who have been separated for months, or even years, literally run toward one another at a full sprint. Sometimes, moms are holding babies who were born during dad's deployment, so we witness daddy and baby meeting for the first time! Smiles, tears, and squeals of joy come from both the dads and the kids. God is a Father like that. If you believe in Jesus's death, burial, and resurrection in your place, you have an eternally secure relationship of love with your Father. And when you get home to Him someday, He'll embrace you like all

---

[53] See Mark 10:13–16.

those soldier dads greet their kids—with passion, love, delight, and joy!

Heavenly Father,
Thank you for your overflowing, passionate love for me.
Thank you that you rejoice over me and take delight in me.
Thank you for sending Jesus do die in my place
so that You and I can be together forever.
Please send the Holy Spirit to bring healing
to the places of my heart that feel unlovable.
In Jesus's Name,
Amen.

6

My Heavenly Father
Wants to Hear from Me

My dad didn't listen to me.

"You still aren't listening to me!" Rachel yelled before slamming the phone down in frustration. Her parents were in the middle of a divorce. Not surprisingly, Rachel felt confused, hurt, and caught in the middle. Her dad was now living apart from the family in his own rented apartment. On several occasions, Rachel had tried to tell her dad how she was feeling, but he wouldn't listen. Admittedly, Rachel's dad was experiencing and processing his own emotions about the divorce. However, when Rachel tried to express her feelings or ask questions, her dad responded with defensiveness instead of engaging with Rachel in a conversation. Rachel admits that there were times that she spoke to her dad in a way that was harsh or accusatory, but she had hoped that her dad could have seen past her outbursts and been willing to talk things out. She wished he understood that she was just a young woman who was hurting and confused about her family splitting up.

Rachel finally asked her dad if they could go see a counselor together, hoping that an objective third party mediating the conversation could help them make some progress. He agreed to go, but the counseling didn't help. Their relationship was a stalemate for the next couple of years. They eventually agreed to sit down with a counselor again. This time, Rachel felt more optimistic and more protected, as she was now married and her husband attended the meeting with her. Unfortunately, this meeting with a counselor was worse than the first one. Rachel's dad brought with him several pages of typed notes that listed all the ways he believed he was a good dad. Instead of talking with her dad, Rachel felt as if she was facing an attorney who came to argue his case. Once again, he did not seem interested in hearing what Rachel had to say. And so the stalemate continued.

Desperate Voices and Bad Listeners

I once heard a pastor say something that I think is at the core of each person's desire to be heard: "To listen is to love. To love is to listen."[54] One glance at social media or the news will tell you that we are a culture of people who are desperate for our voices to be heard. People share the minute and often intimate details of their lives on social media. There are protests, rallies, and marches for an array of causes. And when it comes time for an election, the slogan often repeated is "Vote! Make you voice heard!" We long for the connection that comes when we share our feelings and are genuinely listened to by someone else. We are a people who are desperate to be heard, desperate for relationship, desperate to be loved.

Unfortunately, many people (including you and me) are bad listeners at times, and so our desires for love and relationship go unmet. Maybe, like Rachel, your dad was someone who you wanted to communicate and connect with, but he would allow other things to get in the way of that. According to family counselor Roy Anderson, there are several ways that people can undermine their ability to truly listen to what another person is saying:

- Non-attending—not present, no eye contact.
- Editing—you hear only what you want to hear.
- Rehearsing—you are planning what you want to say.
- Analyzing—you interpret what is being said.

---

[54] Anderson, Roy. "Friends for Life." Sermon given at The Trinity Church in Scottsdale, Arizona, on November 18, 2018.

- Daydreaming—your mind wanders.
- Personalizing—you relate what's said to your own life.
- Switching—you change the subject when possible.
- Judging—you find fault and criticize.
- Advising—you tell them what they need to do.
- Interrupting—you change the flow by speaking before they finish.
- Placating—you agree in order to avoid conflict.
- Disagree—you challenge what is said.
- Asking "Why?"—you put the person on the defensive.
- Interrogating—asking too many questions.[55]

All of these actions sabotage one's ability to listen with compassion and interest. They get in the way of connecting with one another, and they oftentimes create more problems than we started with. Instead of growing closer through conversation, we may feel even more alone and distant.

After the meeting in which Rachel's dad brought in his "evidence" showing that he was a good dad, she began to realize his failure to listen had impacted other areas of her life. Rachel had unfortunately taken on some of his "bad listening" traits over the years. She was a "personalizer," often turning someone else's hurts around and saying, "I've felt that way too. Let me tell you my story." She was an "interrupter," cutting others off before they had said all that was on their heart. Rachel was also a "daydreamer" and struggled to focus on the conversation at hand and not have her mind wander to things she would rather be doing. As a result, Rachel was not experiencing the closeness that she desired in the relationships in her life. Ironically, Rachel didn't experience her dad's love through his listening, and she in turn treated others the same way.

Rachel's view of God as a Father had also become distorted in that she subconsciously believed that He was like her dad. She believed that God the Father didn't really care to listen to her either. She often thought, "God has so many things to attend to in the uni-

---

[55] Ibid.

verse, why would He listen to me? And if He doesn't want to listen to me, does He really even love me?"

The Great Listener

In his book *Life Together,* Dietrich Bonhoeffer says, "Christians have forgotten that the ministry of listening has been committed to them by Him who is Himself the great listener and whose work they should share."[56] God is indeed the Great Listener because "to listen is to love. To love is to listen" and "God is love."[57] Sometimes we can be reluctant to share our thoughts and feelings with others because we aren't sure how they will react, but the Bible tells us that God listens to us with great interest. "The eyes of the LORD are toward the righteous and his ears toward their cry... When the righteous cry for help, the LORD hears and delivers them out of all their troubles."[58] The Father's eyes and ears are toward you in attentive, active listening. What a comfort that is! In God, we always have a ready, willing, and interested Listener. You are God's beloved daughter, and when you belong to Him through Christ, He desires to listen to you. He delights to listen to you. The result is that you feel even more connected to Him, more secure in His love, and your relationship grows stronger.

Another reason we may be reluctant to share our thoughts and feelings with others is that we are afraid of being vulnerable. This can be true especially when that person has been a bad listener for quite some time, as in the case with Rachel's dad. But in God the Father, we have a Listener who treats us with deep compassion and kindness. "For the LORD hears the needy."[59] God is compassionate and tender toward our needs and weaknesses, so we need not fear being vulnerable. He is near, and He hears when we call out to him.

In God the Father, our deepest desires for being heard and being loved are met. We want the connection that comes with sharing our

---

[56] Bonhoeffer, Dietrich. *Life Together,* 98–99.
[57] 1. John 4:8
[58] Psalm 34:15, 17
[59] Psalm 69:33

thoughts and feelings and having them listened to by someone else. The Father does that. We want someone to be our tender and faithful companion in our struggles to help us endure them or find solutions to them. God the Father does that. Other times, we want someone else to share in our joy when we are blessed! God the Father does that too. Your Father is the Great Listener who never tires of hearing your voice raised up to Him.

Talking to Your Father

Before God can listen to us, we must first call out to Him. Our talking to God and His listening to us are like two sides of the same coin. We want someone to hear us out, to validate us, to sympathize with us. Those who don't know God seek these things from others—friends, relatives, online communities—instead of from God Himself. Even those of us who do belong to God often forget that the best person to talk to is God the Father. So often our first reaction is to call, text, or email someone else. Asking a wise and trusted friend is not a bad thing, but we should go to God first. No one listens to us like God does. No one can love us, reassure us, help us, or heal us like He can.

Psalm 55 is a great example of how to talk to God. Here we have King David talking to God after he was betrayed by his friend and counselor, Ahithophel.[60] David pleads to God for mercy, begs for an answer. He says, "I am restless in my complaint, and I moan… My heart is in anguish within me; the terrors of death have fallen upon me. Fear and trembling come upon me, and horror overwhelms me."[61] David holds nothing back. He releases a torrent of thoughts and emotions before the Lord. Instead of seeking out others or stuffing his emotions down, David bears all before God. David seems to know that only God's listening, only God's presence, can provide depth of love and healing he longs for. David continues, "But I call to God, and the LORD will save me. Evening and morning and at noon

---

[60] See 2 Samuel 15:12, 16:23.
[61] Psalm 55:2, 4–5

I utter my complaint and moan, and he hears my voice."[62] He exemplifies 1 Thessalonians 5:17 which tells us to "Pray without ceasing." Morning, noon, and night, as David goes about his days, he cries out to God. It is as if David's heart is a bucket full to the brim of anguish, struggle, and fear; and he pours it out before God until is it empty at last, confident that God will help him. And God lovingly, attentively listened to it all. And He'll listen to you, too, so pour out your bucket to Him. Every last drop.

But How Do I Pray?

I mentioned in the Introduction to this book that some years ago, my pastor preached a sermon series in which we studied how Jesus prayed during his life on earth so that we could learn pray like him too.[63] My pastor said that one of the best ways to learn to pray is to watch a child talk with their dad. Jesus obviously shows us this, as He was the only Son of God praying to His Father. Instead of feeling encouraged that prayer is at the core just a simple conversation between Father and child, I felt discouraged. I was uncomfortable openly sharing the deepest parts myself, even with God. At that time, I only prayed when I needed something or when I had exhausted all my other options: "God, if you're there, can you do this one thing for me?" I wasn't sure God was listening. I didn't know if He'd respond, but it couldn't hurt to try. My lack of knowing God as my Father was a huge impediment to my prayer life.

In addition to not understanding the nature of our relationship to God as His child, what we have been taught about prayer can also get in the way of communicating freely with God. Some of us may have grown up in a church where prayer was quite formal, with a lot of "thees" and "thous." We were taught that we had to pray a certain way if we wanted go get God's attention. Sometimes churches portray prayer as a duty, something God requires of us as

---

[62] Psalm 55:16–17

[63] Much of the content of this section is gleaned from Mark Driscoll's "Pray Like Jesus" reading plan in the YouVersion app.

Christians, which quite frankly sucks all the joy out of it. Some of us do not pray very often because we don't realize how powerful it can be to share our deepest feelings with God and to receive His loving response. The result of all of these misconceptions is that we either don't pray very much, or we do pray but without a full measure of affection and joy. How do you view prayer with your Father? How has your upbringing and past experiences played a part in that?

The fact is, prayer should be enjoyable. It should be like talking to your dad. And it should be a source of comfort, joy, help, and guidance. Prayer should not be something you feel compelled to do as a duty but something you desire to do to as God's beloved child. As in all relationships, your relationship with your Father is largely built through communication. And that's just what payer is—talking to God and hearing from Him.

Prayer doesn't need to look a certain way. You can pray with your hands folded, on your knees, standing with your hands raised, or lying silently in your bed. You can pray when you're in church, when you're with others, when you're alone, when you're in traffic, when you are working, or when you're paying bills. As I mentioned previously, I pray quite often when I'm sweeping the floor! Something about the repetitive motion of sweeping quiets my mind of all of my to-dos and frees me up to talk with my Father. Your prayers can be long, emotional outpourings of your heart, as we saw in Psalm 55 with King David. Or they can be a quick, "Help me, Lord!" You can sing, draw, and journal your prayers. Prayer can even be silently resting in God's presence.

Because we are God's children, the ultimate goal of prayer is to grow our relationship with Him. Think about it this way. My four kids talk to me all day long. Sometimes they need a snack, help finding a certain toy, or for me to get the ball they accidentally threw over the fence. Sometimes, they need to talk because they've been hurt, have a dispute with a sibling, or have woken up in the night with a bad dream. Other times they want to show me a project they made at school or how fast they've gotten on their rollerblades. The point is, we talk all the time about the good, the bad, the hard, the joyful things of life. My kids ask for things they need, share the things they're excited about, and seek comfort and help when they're struggling. As we communicate like this, we build our relationship, and I have the opportunity to teach my children about God and how He loves to listen to them. Praying is a lot like this. As we talk to God about all the things in our life, we build our relationship with Him, and our hearts and our wills become more in tune with His.

Praying to the Father

Praying to God the Father may seem like it should be quite formal, especially if we view Him primarily as Creator, King, or faraway angry old man in the sky. While we should show God reverence, prayer should also be tender. Jesus calls God the Father, "Abba."[64] This was a word that infants would often first call their fathers, much like my kids first said "Dada." Though their speech is awkward at first, little kids learn how to talk by practicing. Before my kids were even old enough to know much about their daddy or have an informed knowledge of how he feels about them, they had an implicit trust because of his lovingkindness toward them. By Jesus calling the Father "Abba" as well, we see the same kind of personal relational bond between the two of them. What's more is that we as Christians also can call God Abba: "For you did not receive the spirit of slavery to fall back into fear, but you have received the Spirit of adoption as sons, by whom we cry, Abba! Father!"[65] The Holy Spirit dwells in us as believers and wells up in us to cry out to God, "Daddy, I need you!" God the Father already knows what you need, how you feel, and what you've done. And yet He invites you to call on Him as your loving Abba.

---

[64] Mark 14:36
[65] Romans 8:15

Praying through the Son

The Bible tells us, "For there is one God, and there is one mediator between God and men, the man Christ Jesus, who gave himself as a ransom for all."[66] Jesus lived the life of perfect obedience we cannot live. He died the guilty sinner's death that we should have died. And He reconciled us to God the Father. That is, Jesus removed the sin that separated us from the Father and brought us back into a relationship of harmony and love. What is even better is that Jesus's acting on our behalf continues on and on. That is why oftentimes when we pray, we say "in Jesus's name." It is by his power, by what He did on the cross, and by his continual presence before the Father that we pray.

A verse that I have always loved is Hebrews 7:25, "Consequently, he [Jesus] is able to save to the uttermost those who draw near to God through him, since he always lives to make intercession for them." Intercession means that Jesus intervenes on our behalf as believers. Imagine Jesus, standing before the Father on your behalf saying, "She belongs to me." Even when you don't know how to pray, what to pray for, or the entirety of what is going on in your current circumstances, Jesus is praying for you.

Praying by the Spirit

In my own journey to learn how to pray, it was relatively easy for me to grasp that we usually pray to the Father through the power and presence of Jesus the Son. But learning how to pray by the power of the Holy Spirit was the one thing that dramatically changed my prayer life. The shortest distance between two points is a straight line, and the Holy Spirit is that straight line. If I have a problem I don't know how to solve, I ask for the Holy Spirit's wisdom. If I need to be patient, forgive, or show kindness to someone I don't want to, I ask for the Holy Spirit to bear His fruit in me. If I'm afraid, I pray for the Holy Spirit's comfort and peace. If I feel the Holy Spirit's con-

---

[66] 1 Timothy 2:5–6a

viction, I pray for Him to help me walk in repentance. My point is, if you hit a place in your life where you feel stuck and what you need or want to do is beyond your power, the Holy Spirit is the very power of God *in you*. You don't need to have the power; you just need submit to God and allow God's power to flow through you.

Furthermore, the Holy Spirit is there when we just can't put our thoughts and feelings into words. When we are so overwhelmed by the severity or the complexity of a situation that we don't even know how to begin to pray, the Holy Spirit is there to help us. The apostle Paul said, "Likewise the Spirit helps us in our weakness. For we do not know what to pray for as we ought, but the Spirit himself intercedes for us with groanings too deep for words…the Spirit intercedes for the saints according to the will of God. And we know that for those who love God all things work together for good, for those who are called according to his purpose."[67] The Holy Spirit is the power of God in our lives and in our hearts. Just as Jesus lives to make intercession for us, the Holy Spirit does too. What a comfort it is to know that God the Father longs to hear from us, but even if we don't know how to pray, we are still being prayed for by the Son and the Spirit that God would continue to work His good will in our lives.

Whether you had a dad who was a good listener or not, you have a heavenly Father who desires to hear from you. Perhaps like Rachel, your dad didn't take the time to listen to your thoughts and feelings, so you've kept them bottled up for many years. For you especially, I encourage you to follow in David's example and pour out to your heavenly Father everything you've been holding in. Sometimes it can be helpful to write your thoughts in a journal. Somehow seeing them written out in black and white allows you to feel a deeper sense of unburdening. Feel free to hear with your Father your feelings of fear, shame, anxiety, being overwhelmed, or anything else you've been locking away. Thank Him for his presence in your life, His salvation, and His blessing. Ask Him for peace, comfort, healing, and what your next step together looks like. You can talk to Him whenever and

---

[67] Romans 8: 26, 27b, 28

wherever you are. Make time in your life for talking with your Father. He's is ready to listen to you.

Heavenly Father,
I praise you as the great listener that you are.
Thank you that you hear me when I call out to you.
Thank you that I can tell you everything that I'm thinking and feeling.
Thank you, Jesus, for interceding for me.
I pray that you would teach me to
talk to you throughout every day.
In Jesus's name,
Amen.

7

My Heavenly Father Gives Me a Home

My dad didn't give me a home.

Countless books, television shows, and movies have been made based on the classic Cinderella story—a poor, lonely girl finds a handsome prince and suddenly has a bright future as his princess. The story of Ruth in the Bible is perhaps the first recorded "Cinderella story" in all of human history. Ruth went from a penniless foreigner with no one in her life but her mother-in-law to having a family, friends, and a fruitful life because God was looking out for her.

The book of Ruth begins by setting a grim scene: "In those days there was no king in Israel. Everyone did what was right in his own eyes."[68] This included intermarrying with people from surrounding nations and worshipping their false gods. This is how Ruth met her husband. There was a famine in the land of Bethlehem, where God's people lived. Bethlehem ironically means "house of bread." Most commentators believe that this famine was a consequence of God's people refusing to follow Him. A man named Elimelech brought his wife Naomi and their two sons, Mahlon and Chilion, from the land that God gave to His people to a foreign land called Moab. This nation began when the incestuous relationship between Lot and one of his daughters' produced a son named Moab. Furthermore,

---

[68] Judges 21:25

73

the Moabites worshiped a false god named Chemosh. The move to Moab may have given Elimelech a better opportunity to put food on the table for his family, but removing them from their home with God's people was not wise. While he undoubtedly was trying to save his family, he brought trouble on them instead.

After Elimielech died, his sons did what was forbidden for God's people and took Moabite wives. Mahlon married Ruth, and Chilion married Orpah. After about ten years, both Mahlon, which means "sick," and Chilion, which means "wasting away," died just as their father had. Nowadays it is normal for women to work and support themselves but not in that day. Naomi, Ruth, and Orpah were in trouble and needed to find a way to provide for themselves. At that time, Naomi heard that "the LORD had visited his people and given them food."[69] As she prepared to go back to Bethlehem, Naomi told her daughters-in-law to return to their parents' homes. There wasn't anything Naomi could to do to help them or provide for them. Orpah chose to return home, but Ruth didn't. Ruth chose to journey to Bethlehem with Naomi.

The Bible doesn't say anything specific about Ruth's parents or family, but I don't think it's too presumptuous to assume that it wasn't a great situation. Why else would she travel with her mother-in-law to a foreign land where she would be seen as an outsider? There was no guarantee of where they would live, how they would support themselves, or if Ruth would even be accepted into the community of God's people. Naomi was in a pretty bad state herself, blaming the Lord for all that she lost in Moab.[70] Yet Ruth chose to stay with Naomi, promising to live and die by her side and to worship her God.[71] With no home, no community, and no family except a bitter mother-in-law, Ruth set out with Naomi to go to where God was blessing His people.

Ruth's situation is not all that different from one in which many women find themselves today. The average age for a woman's first

---

[69] Ruth 1:6
[70] Ruth 1:13
[71] Ruth 1:16–18

marriage was right around twenty years of age from the 1940s until the 1970s, at which point the number began a steady increase. The average woman is now nearly twenty-eight years old when she first marries.[72] I can empathize with Ruth's situation because I was exactly twenty-eight when I met my husband. My parents divorced and sold our family home right before I graduated from college, and I didn't meet my husband until several years later. In those in-between years, I remember feeling very alone and untethered. I had no family home to be a part of anymore, and I hadn't yet met my husband and made a new home with him. Being alone, as Ruth and I both were, is definitely not God's design. God is a Father who wants his kids to dwell with him in a close, loving, enjoyable family relationship; and that should be reflected here on earth, whether they marry or not.

In addition to getting married later in life, divorce is another reason women today often find themselves facing a major transition, just as Ruth did. Although divorce is becoming less common for younger adults ages twenty-five to thirty-nine (partly due to getting married at an older age), "so-called "gray divorce" is on the rise: Among US adults aged fifty and older, the divorce rate has roughly doubled since the 1990s.[73] Even women who remarry are more likely to get divorced again "since remarriages tend to be less stable than first marriages."[74] Though I haven't experienced divorce as a wife, I have as a daughter. And I know enough to empathize with anyone going through it. Divorce is a complicated, emotional, and tumultuous experience for everyone involved.

Another factor contributing to women today perhaps finding themselves without a family or "home" is life expectancy. Women typically live about five years longer than men.[75] I think of my grandparents, who have been married for sixty-six years. They still hold hands, call one another sweet names, and bicker when they play Scrabble. They have been best friends since they were teenagers. To

---

[72] https://www.census.gov/data/tables/time-series/demo/families/marital.html

[73] http://www.pewresearch.org/fact-tank/2017/03/09/led-by-baby-boomers-divorce-rates-climb-for-americas-50-population/

[74] Ibid.

[75] https://www.cdc.gov/nchs/data/nvsr/nvsr66/nvsr66_06.pdf

think of them separated by death (until they reunite in heaven!) is truly heartbreaking.

All of these statistics show that Ruth's story is not out of date but timeless. For one reason or another, women nowadays are often in a similar situation to Ruth's where they are alone and facing major life transitions. However, we can take great comfort in the fact that God didn't leave Ruth alone, and He doesn't leave us alone either. Psalm 68 says, "A father to the fatherless, a defender of widows, is God in his holy dwelling. God sets the lonely in families."[76] Remember, God is a Father who wants his kids to dwell with Him in a close, loving, enjoyable family relationship—not just someday in heaven but here on earth too. Ruth's story shows us three ways that God the Father gives His daughters a home.

A Home with God's People

Let's get back to the story of Ruth and Naomi. They arrived in Bethlehem at the beginning of the barley harvest.[77] When harvesting the grain, workers were told to leave the corners of the field untouched, and if they dropped any bundles of grain, they were not to pick them up. These sections of the field were left for the poor, orphans, widows, and sojourners. Ruth set out to find a field in which to glean to obtain food for her and Naomi. Gleaning was tedious work, as I learned recently on a trip to a local farm that grows wheat, barley, and rye. Ruth would have had to basically crawl on her hands and knees while picking individual grains of barley that had fallen to the ground after the workers came through ahead of her. This was not a high-yield endeavor.

In God's providence, Ruth ended up a field belonging to a man called Boaz. Not only was Boaz a relative of Naomi's (through her husband Elimelech), but he was also a wealthy, respected business-man in the community. Boaz seems to have been an effective leader as well, for even before he personally met Ruth, his workers had allowed

---

[76] Psalm 68:5–6a (NIV)
[77] Ruth 1:22

her to glean all day long. Ruth was humble, hardworking, and would no doubt have been content with gleaning food for her and Naomi, yet Boaz blessed her further. He not only let her glean but instructed his young men not to touch her, ensuring her physical safety. Boaz gave Ruth food and water and even had his workers leave extra grain behind that she could gather. Boaz went above and beyond what the Mosaic Law required him to do for Ruth as a Moabite widow. He treated her according to her need instead of her status as a foreigner.

This type of one-on-one interaction between Ruth and Boaz is often how people still first experience God's people and thus God Himself. My husband and I have been in ministry for over ten years now and most of the time that we see new people come to our church, it's because a friend, coworker, family member, or neighbor invited them. Our relationships with others are a primary way that people can learn what God is like and feel welcome to join His family. We can help them in tough times, as Boaz did with Ruth, and we can celebrate with them in times of blessing. We see this in Ruth's story, for at the end of the book, her relationship with Boaz became a gateway into having a relationship with all of the women in the community. No longer alone, Ruth found family and friends to share her life with. If you are not part of a church family, I would encourage you to find a church home where the Bible is preached and relationships are warm and life-giving. Ruth found a home among God's people and you can too.

A Home of Our Own

At this point in the story of Ruth and Boaz, it feels as if we're watching a romantic comedy knowing the two main characters will end up together even though they don't know it yet! When Ruth returned home and Naomi learned that it was Boaz's field that Ruth had been gleaning in, she was thrilled.

It is important to understand that Boaz was a kinsman-redeemer in Naomi's family. There was a Hebrew custom that if a man died without an heir, his surviving brother was to marry the widow and produce children to continue the family line. The man's land could also be "redeemed" in this way and thus kept in the family. In the book of Ruth, we see these two practices combined into one. As a relative of Naomi's, Boaz was in a position to redeem Ruth through marriage, thus bringing both women into his family.

Naomi had been quite bitter up to this point in the story, but I like to imagine the moment when Ruth told her about gleaning in Boaz's field. This was their chance! They wouldn't have to accept a life of poverty and struggle because Boaz was in a position to change all that. I wonder if her face lit up. Maybe she even let out a little yelp or a chuckle. Maybe she was just dumbstruck. Perhaps she had begun to realize that God had not abandoned them but was still with them, watching out for them. Seizing this amazing opportunity, Naomi devised a plan.

Naomi told Ruth to get dressed up and go down to the threshing floor where Boaz would be after the barley harvest was completed. She then told Ruth to wait to reveal her presence until after Boaz had eaten and drunk. Naomi was no dummy; she wanted Boaz to be completely satisfied and relaxed when Ruth approached him. Ruth did as she was instructed. Once Boaz, was asleep, Ruth gently pulled back his cloak from his feet and waited until he woke up. "At midnight the man [Boaz] was startled and turned over, and behold, a woman lay at his feet!" Now was Ruth's chance! She said, "I am Ruth, your servant. Spread your wings over your servant, for you are a redeemer."[78] Though Ruth was asking Boaz to marry her, this image of spreading his wings over her in protection also recalls the mention of the Lord's "wings" providing Ruth refuge earlier in the book when she ended up in Boaz's field.[79] Boaz wasn't the closest relative in the position of kinsman-redeemer, so Boaz first asked that guy if he wanted to marry Ruth, noting that he'd be marrying a Moabite widow and he'd get a mother-in-law thrown in as a wedding gift. Strategic negotiating on Boaz's part, to be sure. Not surprisingly, the other guy turned him down. So Boaz married Ruth, and God blessed them with a son named Obed. Obed became "the father of Jesse, the

---

[78] Ruth 3:9
[79] Ruth 2:12

father of David," and eventually even Jesus Christ would come from this family line.[80]

My experience is similar to Ruth's. My husband and I are best friends and have a fun and enjoyable marriage. We have four rowdy kids who do not lack in personality! As my husband likes to say, "We bring a party wherever we go!" Even though it has taken me many years to learn what God the Father is like, I feel I have a second chance to experience a dad's relationship to his kids as I watch my husband love, guide, instruct, and enjoy our kids. His family lineage is a strong chain like Boaz's. By God's grace, his parents, his grand-parents, and his great-grandparents love God and have raised their kids to do the same.

My family chain is a bit more like Ruth's, perhaps not completely broken but weak in spots. If it weren't for God's loving, providential hand guiding me to a good church and making me one of his children, I wouldn't have met my husband. It was God's providence—His loving orchestration of events—that led Ruth to Boaz's field. God intervened in my life as well, though in a much more embarrassing way. The only reason I started coming to church again after my wild college years was that I gave my phone number to a guy in a bar and he invited me to church. I liked him, so I went. I only dated that guy for a few weeks, but it was in that church that I heard the Bible preached and felt the Holy Spirit stir something up in my heart. I knew I was in the place I needed to be, and I've continued to grow in the Lord since that day over sixteen years ago. Truth be told, I shudder to think where I would be in life or who I would have married if God hadn't intervened when I did a dumb thing. Instead I get to rejoice that He gave me grace, love, provision, and a new family line and legacy, just like He did for Ruth. Some of you have also and will also experience God providentially altering the course of your life and giving you your own home.

---

[80] Ruth 4:17; Matthew 1:5

An Eternal Home

In the story of Boaz redeeming Ruth (which included Naomi's land and legacy), there was an exchange of money.[81] Through making payment, Boaz took possession of the family's land and the responsibility of marrying Ruth. This is a foreshadowing of what Jesus later came to do. Romans 6:23 says, "For the wages of sin is death, but the free gift of God is eternal life in Christ Jesus our Lord." Jesus is God the Son, who came to earth in human flesh, to stand in our place and pay the death price for our sin, once for all time.[82] Because He did that for us, we are no longer on our own, nor are we in danger of being overtaken by the great enemy, Satan. Now and forever, we belong to God as his beloved daughters, and we wait for "the reappearing of our great God and Savior Jesus Christ" to bring us home to our Father.[83] Like Ruth, we belong to the legacy of Christ and the family of God no matter what our human family lineage is like. Because of Jesus, we are a part of God's eternal family, and our destiny is to be with Him now and forever.

Because Jesus redeemed us, we will have a literal, eternal home with God. Jesus tells us what this will be like: "In my Father's house are many rooms. If it were not so, would I have told you that I go to prepare a place for you? And if I go and prepare a place for you, I will come again and take you to myself, that where I am you may be also."[84] Jesus didn't say that the Father has a kingdom or a city, though He will have those. But in relation to us, we ought to think of eternity with God in terms of a dad preparing a beautiful house that He will live in with His kids.

When I think of this, I remember going to my grandparents' house every summer. We'd pack up the car and drive for two days from Washington state to California. As a child, that two-day drive felt like it would never end! But when we got to Papa's house, it was all worth it: he would stock the deep-freeze in the garage with Fudgsicles,

---

[81] Ruth 4:9–10
[82] Hebrews 9:26
[83] Titus 2:13
[84] John 14:2–3

drag the board games out of storage, and set up the ping-pong table in the side yard. One year when the summer Olympics were taking place, we had our own Ping Pong Olympics. I remember all of us marching around the ping-pong table for the "opening ceremonies" and my grandma carried the "Olympic torch," which was really just an upended plunger with some gold wrapping paper as the flame. In his careful and fun preparation for our visit, my papa was showing us something of what God the Father is like. Our visits at Papa's house were times of love, laughter, and making memories. It was a place where my soul felt loved, enjoyed, safe, secure, and at peace. That is what it feels like when our soul has found its home with God.

When we belong to Him, God the Father gives us a home, a home both now and in heaven someday. A home both practically—with family and church family—as well as a home for our soul. I can tell you from experience that you are not alone and you are not an orphan. Your Father loves you. If you do not have a church family, I pray that you'd find one. If your desire is to be married and have children, I pray that God would bring you a man like Boaz. If your soul feels untethered, I pray that you'd come to know deep in your soul that you belong to your Father and your home is with Him.

Heavenly Father,
Thank you that I am not alone
and that I have home with you and your people.
Thank you for sending Jesus to redeem me
through his death, burial, and resurrection on my behalf.
Thank you that you love me so much you gave your only Son
in order to bring me into your family.
Holy Spirit, please remind me
that I am not an orphan but a daughter,
that I have a loving Father, and that I have an eternal home.
In Jesus's name,
amen.

8

My Heavenly Father Dwells with Me

My dad deserted me.

I am the parent who is home with our kids most of the time. I take care of the laundry, cooking, and daily needs of the kids, but it really is my husband who brings life into our home. Daddy is the one who makes pizza on Friday nights and creates scavenger hunts on Saturdays, sending the kids throughout the house solving riddles and giggling the whole way. When he comes home from work each day, all four kids run at him in greeting. He gets hugs from our three girls and a tackle from our son. Daddy sets the emotional tone in our home too. When a child is having a hard time obeying or there is bickering between siblings, he talks through the situation calmly and usually with a creative analogy that helps the kids learn how to navigate whatever their struggle. He's the one who sends them off to bed with prayers and back rubs. He's the one from whom we all gain a sense of safety, security, and joy. He loves us, and he loves being with us. His home is with us and ours is with him, and that will never change. The Bible calls this "dwelling" with one another. That is, living and being settled in a place together. My kids are not afraid that one day Daddy will choose to leave and make his home somewhere else. In fact I'd be willing to bet that that thought has never even entered their minds. Our relationship with God the Father ought to be and can be like that: He's a Father who will never leave, and you don't need to be afraid that He will.

Our earthly dads are supposed to show us that the Father is our Dad who will always be with us, but unfortunately many dads distort our view of the Father by abandoning us to one degree or another. When it is our dad who leaves us, a fear that God will do the same lodges deep in our soul and keeps us from closeness with Him. Out of fear and attempted self-preservation, we will not draw near to a God who we believe will abandon us.

Meant to Dwell

Despite our fear or uncertainty, the truth is that God the Father is absolutely incapable of abandoning you. As I've mentioned in a previous chapter, the most frequent promise that God makes to us in the Bible is "I will be with you." Before people sinned, before we needed forgiveness, before we needed anything else, we were promised God's presence because He made us for life with Him. We were made to live in relationship with Him like my kids live with and share their lives with their daddy. We were made to dwell with God.

Going back to the creation of Adam and Eve in Eden, we see that God walked in the garden with them in the cool of the day. I live in Arizona, and I finally understand what "cool of the day" means. We like to take family walks in the cool of the day when the burning sun is finally setting, illuminating the sky in reds, pinks, and purples. Imagine taking a sunset walk with God. Adam and Eve probably did! However, the beautiful closeness of Adam and Eve dwelling with God was ruined when they sinned, and indeed our sin separates us from Him as well. Adam and Eve's sin was like a wedge that broke the relationship apart, so God made them leave the garden. This may sound harsh, but think of it another way. A godly dad makes rules and guidelines for his kids to live by so that they can grow and flourish. We have three main rules in our house: Be safe. Have fun. Love each other. A godly dad also locks the doors at night to protect his kids and keep the home a place of safety and peace. God is a Father like that. He wants us to live with Him and obey what He says because He knows how life works best. Furthermore, He wants to enjoy life with us, but He cannot dwell where sin does because He is holy. This means that God is completely separate and set apart from anything sinful, evil, profane, or unclean. We'll explore more about God's holiness in another chapter.

Despite Adam and Eve's sin that separated them from God, His desire to dwell with them did not diminish. But how would this be accomplished? How would the broken relationship be mended? How could the sin that separated them be removed? Immediately after the heartbreaking moment when He cast Adam and Eve out of the garden, God proclaimed the coming of Jesus, who would eventually restore our dwelling relationship.[85] By dying in our place on the cross, Jesus would take our punishment for sin and thereby remove the barrier between us and the Father. The Father knows we could never pay off our own debt of sin, yet He desires so much to dwell with us that He sent Jesus to pay the debt for us. Even when people sinned, God remained a God who dwells. He is not a God who leaves.

The Tent of God's Dwelling

Before Jesus came, God had promised (made a covenant) to dwell with his people, but there were limitations on experiencing his presence. The book of Hebrews gives us a helpful summary of that first covenant:

> That first covenant between God and Israel had regulations for worship and a place of worship here on earth. There were two rooms in that Tabernacle. In the first room were a lampstand, a table, and sacred loaves of bread on the table. This room was called the Holy Place. Then there was a curtain, and behind the curtain was the second room called the Most Holy Place. In that room were a gold incense altar and a wooden

---

[85] Genesis 3:15

chest called the Ark of the Covenant, which was covered with gold on all sides. Inside the Ark were a gold jar containing manna, Aaron's staff that sprouted leaves, and the stone tablets of the covenant. Above the Ark were the cherubim of divine glory, whose wings stretched out over the Ark's cover, the place of atonement. But we cannot explain these things in detail now.

When these things were all in place, the priests regularly entered the first room as they performed their religious duties. But only the high priest ever entered the Most Holy Place, and only once a year. And he always offered blood for his own sins and for the sins the people had committed in ignorance. By these regulations the Holy Spirit revealed that the entrance to the Most Holy Place was not freely open as long as the Tabernacle and the system it represented were still in use.[86]

Between the cherubim on the mercy seat is where God would manifest His glory and meet with his people.[87] And that was kept in the Most Holy Place where only the high priest could go once per year. In addition, these repeated animal sacrifices only dealt with outward cleansing and were not able to cleanse the consciences of the people.[88] This means there was still the separation of sin keeping God from being in an unhindered, intimate dwelling relationship with His people. People's hearts still hadn't been cleansed from sin and made new. For that, we needed Jesus.

---

[86] Hebrews 9:1–8 (NLT)
[87] Exodus 25:22
[88] Hebrews 9:9–10

The Word Became Flesh

Just as God had promised back in Genesis 3:15, Jesus came to restore and forever secure our ability to dwell in close relationship with God. John 1:14 says, "And the Word Became flesh and dwelt among us, and we have seen his glory, glory as of the only Son from the Father, full of grace and truth." There is that *dwell* word. This is huge. No longer was God's presence only manifest behind the curtain of the Most Holy Place and available only to the high priest once a year. God the Father sent God the Son to earth, in flesh, so anyone and everyone could see him, talk to him, touch him, and spend time with him.

Unlike false religions and spiritualities that say people need to put forth effort to get to their god, our God—the true God—came to dwell with us and to make a way for us to dwell with Him forever. Indeed Hebrews 9:12 says, "With his own blood—not the blood of goats and calves—He [Jesus] entered the Most Holy Place *once for all time* and secured our redemption forever" (emphasis mine). In fact, at the moment of Jesus's death, the curtain of the temple that separated the Most Holy Place was literally torn in two from top to bottom. We often think of a veil as the thin, transparent covering a bride wears over her head at a wedding, but this veil was another thing entirely. It would have been between forty-five and sixty feet high and perhaps four inches thick.[89] Furthermore, the fact that the veil tore from top to bottom leaves no doubt that power that ripped through this wall of separation came from above. God alone brought an end to the separation between Him and those who believe in Jesus's death on their behalf.

The Indwelling Spirit

Jesus knew He would go back to be with the Father instead of remaining on earth, but that didn't mean that God's presence would depart for heaven as well. Jesus prepared His disciples for His ascen-

---

[89] https://www.compellingtruth.org/temple-veil-torn.html

sion back in heaven by telling them of the coming Holy Spirit. He said, "If you love me, you will keep my commandments. And I will ask the Father and he will give you another Helper to be with you forever… You know him, for he *dwells* with you and will be in you" (emphasis mine).[90] Jesus promised to anyone who loves him and obeys him, "my Father will love him, and we will come to him and make our home with him."[91]

The apostle Paul also wrote of the indwelling Holy Spirit: "Or do you not know that your body is a temple of the Holy Spirit within you, whom you have from God?"[92] The Greek word used here for *temple* was used as the sacred part of the physical temple in Jerusalem, meaning the Holy Place and the Most Holy Place. It is also used metaphorically to describe "the spiritual temple consisting of the saints of all ages joined together by and in Christ."[93] Because of the death, burial, and resurrection of Jesus to remove the sin that separates us from the Father, the physical temple in Jerusalem is now no longer the place where God's Spirit dwells. Now He dwells in us as believers!

Do you see the progression of God dwelling with his people? Adam and Eve dwelt with God in the garden until they sinned and broke the relationship. But God continued to dwell with his people, manifesting his presence behind the curtain of the Most Holy Place. When Jesus came and died in our place for our sin, however, that curtain was permanently torn in two, opening up a way for us to be with God again. And after Jesus ascended back into heaven, the Father sent the Holy Spirit to "dwell" inside of us! What could be better than the power of God Himself dwelling in our hearts?[94]

But there is still something even better on the horizon. Jesus will come back one day to bring us back to the Father[95] where we'll physically dwell with him forever. (We'll talk about this in much greater detail in another chapter.) In fact, the Holy Spirit dwelling

---

90 John 14:15–16,17b
91 John 14:23
92 1 Corinthians 6:19
93 https://www.blueletterbible.org/lang/lexicon/lexicon.cfm?Strongs=G3485&t=ESV
94 Romans 8:11
95 John 14:18

in us is our guarantee that this will in fact happen.[96] He lives in us to walk with us day by day, to encourage us, instruct us, and guide us, and bear fruit in us until the day when Jesus comes back to bring us home to the Father. The beautiful image of God walking in the Garden of Eden with his people in the cool of the day will once again, and for all eternity, be restored.

> *Heavenly Father,*
> *Thank you that you choose to dwell with me.*
> *Thank you for sending Jesus to die and rise*
> *for my sin so that there is no longer anything*
> *separating us from dwelling with one another.*
> *Please send the Holy Spirit to help me*
> *be aware today of your indwelling presence in my heart.*
> *Thank you that Jesus will come back one day to bring me home to You.*
> *In Jesus's name,*
> *amen.*

---

[96] 2 Corinthians 1:22

PART 2

Destructive Dads

9

My Heavenly Father Is Light

My dad was dark.

I woke up this morning to the most beautiful sunrise. The back of our house faces east and has huge windows, so every morning I watch as the sky changes. When I first wake up, all I see is the blackness of night. But slowly, light begins to streak through the darkness. First, the sky changes from black to a deep inky blue. Then comes the watercolor effect of pink and orange and purple. Finally, the bright blue sky of the day arrives. This morning one of my children noticed the bright-orange sky and exclaimed, "Look, look!" The other three children dashed to the window, and a collective, "Wow!" followed. We live in Arizona, so we get a blessed three hundred days of sunshine each year, and I'm thankful for every single sunrise.

Before we came to Arizona, we lived in Washington state, a place that has roughly as many sunny days as overcast days every year. I'm not talking about the kind of weather that is cloudy, but you can still see sun breaks. I'm talking about a heavy ceiling of thick gray clouds. Each year as the Seattle summer would draw to a close and fall settled in, I braced myself for the coming season of darkness. Between October and March, sometimes even into April, the weather forecast was usually somewhat cold and mostly overcast. To make matters worse, the sun officially goes down in the winter around 4:30 p.m. On a day that the sun really never comes out, it feels almost like perpetual darkness. Maybe I'm more sensitive to the gloomy weather than other people, and I sound a bit melodramatic, but the contrast between sunny light and gloomy darkness felt very real to me. It was just depressing for months on end. One day during our last winter in Washington, I remember sitting on the edge of the bed sobbing in the middle of the afternoon. (Full disclosure, I was newly pregnant with my fourth child, so hormones no doubt played a part in my emotional state.) I just longed for a clear, sunny day. When we told our family and friends that we were moving to Arizona, they would often say, "But it's so hot there!" Oh yes, it's a triple-digit, furnace hot from June through September, but glory be it is so, so sunny.

There is something in the way God made us to love the light. It's why people go on vacations to hot, sunny places. It's why all kinds of birds flock to Arizona for the winter. We welcome snowbirds every autumn: ducks, geese, and others that come from colder, darker climates to spend the winter and spring here and give birth to a new generation of feathered friends. A couple years ago, a daddy and mommy duck chose our yard as the place where they'd welcome their new brood. They made a nest behind one of our palm trees, and when those babies hatched, the mother duck taught them to swim in our pool. Our kids thought it was the greatest thing that had ever happened to them. Nature right in our own yard!

We have another kind of "snowbird" in Arizona as well: people who come to enjoy the sun, golf courses, and outdoor living of winter in the desert. Instead of shoveling snow in their driveway, these fine folks enjoy hiking, golfing, and dining outside in the middle of November. I know exactly when they arrive every year because it becomes nearly impossible to find a parking spot at my local Costco. All this to say, we were made by the God of Light to love the light ourselves.

Light and Dark in the Bible

Genesis 1:2 declares, "The earth was without form and void, and darkness was over the face of the deep. And the Spirit of God was hovering over the face of the waters."[97] And then, in the first of

---

[97] Genesis 1:2

God's acts of creation, He said, "'Let there be light', and there was light. And God saw that the light was good. And God separated the light from the darkness."[98] Before anything else in creation, God made light. Light is so crucial to our existence that God made it before anything else. Think about it—almost everything in the natural world needs light. Light is essential for life, health, and growth. Plants need light for photosynthesis, the process by which they convert carbon dioxide and water into food. Sunlight also plays a role in flowering and pollination of plants. Many animals rely on sunlight to raise their body temperatures. For people, sunlight plays a key role in people's ability to make vitamin D, which helps our bodies to absorb nutrients, regulate nerve signaling, and support our immune system.[99]

The same need for light in the physical world exists in the spiritual world as well. Just as a flower needs light to survive, so, too, does the health of your soul depend on the light that comes from God and relationship with Him. Light brings life and health. Psalm 56:13 says that when we walk with God, we walk "in the light of life." Jesus himself said, "I am the light of the world. Whoever follows me will not walk in darkness but will have the light of life." Just as the natural world depends on light, just as we feel a surge of energy when the sun is shining on our face, our soul receives life from the light that comes from God.

Light also illuminates our path so we can see where we are going, both literally and spiritually. This is why we have headlights on our cars. If not for those beams in the night, we'd drive off the road or crash into another vehicle. God, particularly through His Word in the Bible, gives light to guide our lives. Psalm 119:105 says, "Your word is a lamp to my feet and a light to my path." Jesus himself said, "If anyone walks in the day he does not stumble, because he sees the light of this world."[100] God's Word guides us in making decisions in life when we don't know what to do, especially when we don't fully

---

98 Genesis 1:3–4
99 https://www.livestrong.com/article/13719526-vitamin-d/
100 John 11:9

understand a situation, which happens quite often! God knows all, sees all, and will guide us to do what is best for us. We can trust the Father to light our path.

Light also brings safety. We are naturally afraid of the unknown. As children, we were perhaps afraid of the dark at bedtime. As adults, we are afraid in situations or relationships in which things are hidden from us, "kept in the dark," so to speak. Can I trust someone is telling me the whole truth? Why is my company restructuring, and what impact will it have on me? Why did someone I care about do something to hurt me? Are they keeping something from me? What are they not telling me? Light brings safety because it exposes things that were once hidden in darkness. Ephesians 5:13 tells us, "But when anything is exposed by the light, it becomes visible." Light helps to drive away our fears by making the unknown fully known.

We often hear Christians talk about "living in the light." This comes from 1 John, which was written by the apostle John. He was Jesus's best friend on earth and was an elderly grandpa by the time He wrote this letter.

> God is light; and in him is no darkness at all. If we say we have fellowship with him while we walk in darkness, we lie and do not practice the truth. But if we walk in the light, as he is in the light, we have fellowship with one another, and the blood of Jesus his Son cleanses us form all sin. If we say we have no sin, we deceive ourselves, and the truth is not in us. If we confess our sins [bring them into the light], he is faithful and just to forgive us our sins and to cleanse us from all unrighteousness [101]

Living in the light doesn't mean we have to be perfect. God knows we can't do that. A person who is living in the light will walk in humility, integrity, generosity, openness, repentance, and a clear

---

[101] 1 John 1:5b-9

conscience. When we mess up, we are honest and bring our sin into the light, to the Person who is the Light of the World—Jesus himself. He is the one who cleanses us completely from every sin, stain, and shame. Furthermore, when we walk in the light where God is, we will have a close, loving, thriving relationship with Him and with others. Living in the light doesn't mean that we'll be perfect and never stumble into the darkness, but it does mean that we will quickly return to the God of Light and will not keep any corner of our lives hidden from Him.

There is a difference between keeping something secret and keeping some time private. A secret is something that I keep hidden, that I don't want anyone else to see or speak into. Keeping something secret often happens when we are embarrassed, ashamed, or afraid of losing something even though we might know that it's not good for us. Some examples would be an unhealthy relationship that we know we shouldn't be engaged in, a substance abuse, pornography addiction, obsession with weighing oneself, provocative shows or movies, or even fantasies that we entertain in our mind. Secrets are bad things that are kept from the light. They are often destructive because the most dangerous sins are the secret ones.

In contrast, private things are, frankly, things that simply aren't other people's business. For example, my husband and I don't tell others every detail of what we say and do together as a couple. We do have trusted pastors and friends that we can talk about intimate things with, but we don't share them with everyone. That is how privacy works. Some people get to know but not everyone. Walking in the light doesn't mean that everyone has to know everything about us and our lives. It is good to only share private things with a few safe people you trust and who have your best interests in mind.

Darkness Hates the Light

Darkness, obviously, is the opposite of light. Instead of having a relationship with God and receiving his guidance to light our path in life, those who walk in darkness "are darkened in their understanding, alienated from the life of God because of the ignorance that is in them, due to their hardness of heart."[102] People who walk in darkness avoid the light for fear of having their dark thoughts and deeds exposed.[103] Their hearts are hard, their minds are dark, and they eventually will stumble.[104] The Bible describes darkness as "orgies, drunkenness, sexual immorality, sensuality, quarreling, jealousy, and fleshly desires" [105] among other things. People who walk in darkness dishonor God and trust in themselves. They do not believe there is ultimate Truth, but that we all get to live by our own truths and perspectives. This is not something new in our day, for Isaiah 5:20 says, "Woe to those who call evil good and good evil." People who walk in darkness do not readily confess when they have done something wrong or voluntarily bring their misdeeds to the light. Rather, they have to get caught, and even then they often only partially confess. Sometimes darkness looks like self-righteousness and justifying one's beliefs or actions, even when they are opposed to God. Furthermore, relationships with these types of people are very complicated because you don't ever know where you stand with them, as they keep their true thoughts and actions hidden.

Those who persist in walking in darkness have no hope for life, for in the end, they will only experience the darkness of death, hell, and eternal separation from God. This is the destiny that God has declared for him who is the source of all darkness—Satan himself. Satan knows he's going to eventually be completely defeated by the Light,[106] and he's trying to take down as many people as he can with him into eternal darkness.

When Dad Is Dark

Sometimes it can be hard to distinguish between light and dark. Just like our eyes adjust to the dark when we're in a movie theater, our soul can adjust to the darkness around us in the world. While

---

[102] Ephesians 4:18
[103] John 3:19–21
[104] John 11:10
[105] Romans 13:12
[106] Revelation 12:12

maintaining our hatred of clear acts of evil, we can become desensitized to lesser acts of darkness—lying, pride, indulgence, laziness. This is precisely why we need God's light. We often don't know what is dark until the light shines on it and exposes it. One of the most disorienting ways we can experience darkness is when it comes from our dad. Dads should help their daughters to feel safe and loved. They should guide our path and be a life-giving presence in their daughter's lives. They should teach us to follow God's ways as well as how to interact with the broken world around us. But some dads bring darkness into our lives in a way that can leave us confused about who God is. This is Sara's story.

Sara has always felt uneasy about her dad. For many years, she felt silly about this uncomfortable feeling. Her dad always provided for the family; he wasn't an alcoholic; and he wasn't violent. He made good money at his nine-to-five job and came home every night for dinner. He also taught children's Sunday school at the church they dutifully attended every Sunday. On paper, he seemed like a great dad, so she felt unjustified about her anxiety. But something about him just always seemed "off." As she got older, Sara began to learn things about the past that finally shed light on her feelings.

Sara remembers when she was a very little girl that her dad got a second job at a grocery store, even though he had a good career. She even remembered how he had to shave off his beard for the job. It may seem like a small detail, but he had always had a beard, so to a little girl, this was a drastic change in her dad. Years later, Sara learned that her dad got the grocery store job to pay off some debts he incurred when he was arrested for stealing merchandise from a local store. She was dumbfounded. Her dad had been arrested, and she had no idea.

Over the years he would show up with a new TV or a new watch and say that he had won them in some contest. But because of her dad's track record, Sarah's mom said she had always been suspicious that these items were actually stolen. Sara also remembered a time when her dad was in a car accident that was the other driver's fault, but it then seemed as if he was taking advantage of the situation to get money out of the other person's insurance company.

The deception didn't end there. Many years later when her parents got divorced, it came to light that her dad had opened credit cards in her mom's name without her knowledge. He had racked up such debt that her parents had to declare bankruptcy while also in the process of getting divorced. Years and years of her dad's operating in darkness had come to light and played a huge role in the destruction of their family.

Sara recalls one time when her confusion and uneasiness had become strong enough that she confronted her dad about his hypocrisy. She saw her dad's Bible on his nightstand, and it was covered in dust. "Dad, why don't you read your Bible anymore?"

He replied, "I've already read it. I know what it says." Maybe he did. But it seemed to Sara that he didn't have a relationship with the One who wrote it.

The trouble with people who act covertly, who operate in darkness, is that even when some things come to light, some things usually remain hidden. Sara has no idea if her dad has any other untold secrets. Did he have any other scrapes with the law? Was he ever unfaithful to her mom? She'll probably never know the full truth.

As I've said many times in this book, your dad is supposed to show you what God the Father is like. So when Dad is displaying both elements of light (providing for the family, going to church) yet also elements of darkness (lying, deception, unrepentance), a daughter can become greatly confused. If Dad is both dark and light, can you really trust the light parts of him? This is how Sara felt. She says she often wondered, "Is my dad truly safe? Does he truly love me? And if my own dad is capable of darkness, how I am I supposed to trust anyone else? How am I supposed to trust God?"

The sun is so bright, so powerful that we can't look directly at it. Yet even the sun in all of its brilliance has dark spots from time to time. For many years, Sara viewed God like that. She believed that He was mostly good, loving and kind, but also that He was disappointed in her. She knew she didn't deserve His love or salvation, so why would He just give it to her as a gift? Yes, God had taken care of and provided for her so far, but would He always? Would He always be light? Would He ever have a dark spot?

God Is Light

First John 1:5 is a verse you might be familiar with: "God is light, in him is no darkness at all." It's one of those verses where many of us know what it says, but we don't always know what it means. No other being in the universe can make this claim or fulfill this characterization. God alone is always and only light. Another word for this would be to say that God is holy. Indeed the Bible's most frequently named attribute of God is "holy." A. W. Tozer explains God's holiness like this:

> We cannot grasp the true meaning of divine holiness by thinking of someone or something very pure and then raising the concept to the highest degree we are capable of. God's holiness is not simply the best we know of infinitely better. We know nothing like divine holiness. It stands apart, unique, unapproachable, incomprehensible and unattainable.[107]

There is no human standard that God conforms to. He is completely outside of and beyond anything we could possibly imagine. He is "King of kings and Lord of lords, who alone has immortality, who dwells in unapproachable light."[108] The purity of God is nothing that we have ever come into contact with in the natural world. Everything He is, He is in holiness: holy love, holy justice, holy faithfulness, holy wisdom, holy mercy, holy grace, and on and on. God is pure light. It's who He is and who He always will be. There has never and will never be a dark spot in Him. This makes him safe, trustworthy, and the source of everything we need for a healthy life.

---

[107] Tozer, A. W., *The Knowledge of the Holy*, 163.
[108] See 1 Timothy 6:15–16

Rescued from the Dark, Forever in the Light

Imagine that you have been taken captive by an evil dragon. Yes, this is a little bit of a fairy-tale vibe, but stick with me. I want you to envision the dragon Smaug from *The Lord of the Rings*. He's as big as a Boeing 747. He's black and thorny; he breathes smoke from his nostrils and fire from his mouth. He's utterly dark, demonic, terrifying. And he's taken you captive and chained you up in his dungeon. You are disoriented, not sure of where you are or how long you've been there. You're weak, scared, and despairing. You have no strength left to fight, no way of getting yourself out of the snares of the dragon or his darkness. Every time you hear a noise at the door of your cell, dreading of who might be coming surges through your soul. The dragon has already starved you, accused you, interrogated you, isolated you, and abused you. What else is left but to take your very life? You feel as if you are without hope.

Just when you fear that the darkness will completely overtake you, there is a banging at the door! You cower into the corner of your cell, pain searing through your body as you hit the stony floor, for you are now mere skin and bones. "Don't be afraid," says a voice. You slowly turn your eyes upward and see his face: a strong, kind hero dressed in white, carrying a sword. Not a hair on his head is out of place, not a drop of blood or dirt is on his cloak. "I'm here to rescue you. You're safe now," he says. And as he calls you by your own name, you know that this is the voice of the One who loves you, who has come to save and rescue you. The voice of the One you were meant to know and be with forever.

You can hardly move for both the physical weakness of your body and the overwhelming relief you now feel in your soul. The hero removes your shackles, gently picks you up, cradles you in a strong yet tender embrace, and marches you straight out of that dungeon, never to return. Your eyes squint reflexively when you get outside into the sunshine; you've been in the darkness so long that the light comes as a shock. Your lungs swell automatically to fill with fresh air. And out of the corner of your eye, you see that the dragon lies motionless on the ground; the mouth that once breathed fire is now toothless and bloody. Your hero notices you staring at the dragon and says, "Don't worry. I'll come back to finish him off later. Let's get you home first." Darkness has been defeated. Light has prevailed. But this is no fairy tale.

Though I've completely made up the details of this story, this is essentially what has happened to humanity. Beginning with Adam and Eve in the Garden of Eden, humanity has been taken captive by Satan, the father of lies and darkness himself. By his deception, every human who has ever lived—except for Jesus—has become a slave to sin. But God the Father sent Jesus to rescue us:

> I am the LORD; I have called you in righteousness; I will take you by the hand and keep you; I will give you as a covenant for the people, a light for the nations; to open the eyes that are blind, to bring out the prisoners from the dungeon, from the prison those who sit in darkness.[109]

> He has delivered us from the domain of darkness and transferred us to the kingdom of his beloved Son.[110]

> For at one time you were darkness, but now you are light in the Lord. Walk as children of the light.[111]

> The LORD will be your everlasting light.[112]

> The light shines in the darkness, and the darkness can never extinguish it.[113]

---

[109] Isaiah 42:6–7
[110] Colossians 1:13
[111] Ephesians 5:8
[112] Isaiah 60:20
[113] John 1:5

God your Father sent Jesus to conquer Satan, sin, and death and to free you from the clutches of darkness once and for all. Colossians 2:15 says, "He [Jesus] disarmed the rulers and authorities and put them to open shame, by triumphing over them in him." If you have placed your faith in Jesus's work on the cross, there is no condemnation for you, no shame to feel. The one who brings shame, Satan, was defeated and openly put to shame himself when Jesus died and rose again. Satan will try his best to continue to tempt, accuse, frighten, and condemn you—to bring you back into the darkness—but his power over you has been destroyed by Jesus. You now belong eternally to your Father. There is no darkness in Him at all. He is Light, His kingdom is light, and you belong to the people of the light. You can let your guard down. Your shackles are gone. You are safe, you are loved, and that will never change. So then, let's walk in our Father's light and share it with our world that so desperately needs it.

Heavenly Father,
I praise you, that you are the source of all Light,
and that there is no darkness in you at all.
Thank you that you have brought me into your kingdom of light
Where I am safe and loved.
I pray that your Spirit would fill me with the light of your presence
and help me to walk in freedom.
In Jesus's name,
amen.

10

My Heavenly Father
Tells the Truth

My dad lied.

Nothing ruins trust in a relationship like lying. There are lies of commission, in which the person says something that is untrue. There are also lies of omission, in which a person leaves out details, fails to disclose the full truth, or distorts the truth. Sometimes lies are big and bring a relationship down all at once, like a dam breaking loose. Other times, small lies drip, drip, drip over time and erode a relationship slowly. In their book *Safe People*, psychologists Dr. Henry Cloud and Dr. John Townsend state, "There is no way a relationship can prosper and grow if one person is a liar."[114]

Ideally, when people are caught in a lie, they will own up to it. Then the truth can come out, and to the degree that the person is willing to repent of their lies and tell the truth, the relationship can move toward reconciliation and healing. Unfortunately, some people stay committed to their lies. When confronted with the truth, they justify their actions, blame-shift, or heap on even more lies in order to avoid telling the truth. Lying means death for a relationship because the deception makes the relationship feel unsafe.

When we find ourselves in a relationship with someone who lies, we respond in various self-protective ways. We begin to distrust

---

[114] Cloud, Dr. Henry and Townsend, Dr. John, *Safe People*. p. 38.

almost everything the other person says or does. We question things they have said and done in the past. We do not make any plans or decisions based on their words. And we do not trust how they feel about us. Because the relationship is no longer safe, we hold back. We are rightly afraid to invest ourselves in a relationship that is toxic. To one degree or another, we stop listening to what the other person is saying because we know we can't fully trust it. We may even shield ourselves from other people, afraid this deception could happen in other relationships as well. Lies are like a wedge that drives people apart, sometimes to the degree that the relationship eventually breaks apart.

A Lying Dad

A dad who lies to us damages our identity as a daughter that is loved, protected, and cared for. As the head of the family, dad is supposed to teach us how to interact with others and think about the world. Our relationship with our dad is also supposed to be kind of a precursor for our relationship with God. As we learn to trust our dad as a father who loves, protects, and guides us with the truth of God's Word, we learn to do the same with God the Father who is the source of that Truth. So when our dad is untruthful, we can't trust what he says about us or the world. We can struggle to trust others as well. Sometimes we even struggle to trust God. We ask ourselves questions such as, "If my dad isn't honest with me, is God honest with me? If my dad holds back helpful advice or information from me, does God do that too? If my dad says one thing but does the opposite, does God do that as well?"

The most important thing we must realize about lies and deception is that they ultimately come from Satan. Jesus himself said as much, "He [the devil] was a murderer from the beginning, and he does not stand in the truth, because there is no truth in him. When he lies, he speaks out of his own character, for he is a liar and the father of lies."[115] Satan's character is that of a liar, and his language is

---

[115] John 8:44

lies. He speaks nothing other than lies. He deceives us. He bends the truth. He hurls false accusations. And he is cunning and crafty. He's not dumb, but he is evil. I'm not saying that a lying dad is necessarily evil. But what I am saying is that lies always and only originate from the enemy. They never originate from God. Yet our relationship with God becomes damaged when we begin to project onto Him the character of our lying dad or of the enemy.

In our minds, we know that God is not a liar. But if we've grown up with a dad who lies or distorts the truth, we can find it very difficult to believe that God the Father doesn't do the same. You might think, "That's crazy. Of course, I know that God doesn't lie or deceive me." But answer this honestly: Are you willing to place *all* of your trust in Him? Do you trust him with every part of your life—your finances, your kids, your relationships, your hurts, fears, and dreams? Do you believe what He says about you—that you are his beloved beautiful daughter? Do you feel secure? Do you feel loved? Are you holding something back in your relationship with God? If your answer is yes to any of these questions, we need to circle back and look at who God is, as well as how and why He speaks to us so that we can truly believe that He only and always tells us the truth.

God Chooses to Speak

Our God is a God who reveals himself. That sounds simple enough, but if you think about it, He didn't have to communicate with us at all. Yet He speaks to us in a variety of ways. One way God reveals himself to us is through creation: "The heavens declare the glory of God and the sky above proclaims his handiwork."[116] He made the entire cosmos, from vast galaxies all the way down to tiny blades of grass, simply by speaking them into existence. Imagine you are looking at a beautiful sunset or the sound of crashing ocean waves. Think about the way a child's giggle stirs up joy in your heart the way the human body can heal from a ravaging disease. Think about how a delicious meal tastes, how perfectly the flavors work

---

[116] Driscoll, Mark, *Doctrine*, 38; Psalm 19:1

together in harmony to produce something utterly satisfying. All of this is God communicating something of Himself to us. He is creative, He is beautiful, He provides for us, He is watching over us, He loves us, and He wants us to enjoy the world He's made. God is communicating all around us; but so often in our busy world full of information, headlines, and opinions, we miss His messages.

If you read through the Old Testament, you'll find some pretty peculiar ways God spoke to people. He spoke to Moses through a burning bush. Jesus came down from heaven in the form of a man and wrestled Jacob in the night. He even spoke to a man named Balaam through a talking donkey. Oftentimes, God appointed prophets, like Moses, Jeremiah, Ezekiel, Habakkuk, and more to speak His words to His people.

God could have continued to speak to us in those ways, but the primary way God speaks to us today is through the Bible. God has put into words we can understand something of the beauty, holiness, and mystery that He is. God so desires us to know Him that He inspired the writing of Scripture. Indeed, the Holy Spirit inspired not just the topics or thoughts of the Bible but every word.

The reason we can believe the Bible as God's truthful word is that God's character is that of truth teller. Hebrews 6:18 says that "it is impossible for God to lie." God tells the truth. It is not in His nature to lie; He's incapable of it. Psalm 119:160 (NLT) says, "The very essence of your words is truth; all your just regulations will stand forever." Because God's character never has and never will change,[117] He will always be a truth teller. He will never be a liar. And we can completely trust all that He says.

Comparing the Bible to other ancient texts reveals even more evidence about its reliability. Most scholars would never question the reliability of texts from Plato, Sophocles, Homer, or Caesar Augustus, but we have fewer than ten copies of each of those books.[118] In the case of the New Testament, we have over 14,000 ancient copies with fragments written no later than one hundred

---

[117] Hebrews 13:8
[118] *Doctrine*, 63.

years after the original books and letters.[119] The variations that do occur in the different copies usually involve spelling, word order, or style because these were all handwritten.[120] Simply put, the Bible *is* reliable. In fact, the Bible is the most reliable ancient text on planet Earth. It is perfect, without error, and is inspired by the Holy Spirit. It is the ultimate authority about God, ourselves, and indeed the whole world.

Another point of confidence in the reliability of the Bible comes when we consider the Old Testament prophesies about the future, including the coming of Jesus. "No other world religion or cult can present any specific prophesies concerning the coming of their prophets. However, in the Old Testament we see hundreds of fulfilled prophecies extending hundreds and sometimes over a thousand years into the future, showing God's foreknowledge of and sovereignty over the future."[121] In Isaiah 55:11 God says, "So shall my word be that goes out from my mouth; it shall not return empty, but it shall accomplish that which I purpose, and shall succeed in the thing for which I sent it." The fact that what God says actually comes to pass gives us confidence that what He says is true.

Despite the rise and fall of nations, religious persecutions, natural disasters, and plain old human error, the Bible is as reliable today as it was when the Holy Spirit inspired the original writing. That in and of itself is a miracle of God. The Bible is both *timely*, applying to life today, and *timeless*, applying to all times, places, and peoples. So strong is God's desire to speak to you that He has caused the written account of His word to be preserved through the ages and to be spread among the nations. The fact that God went to such lengths to preserve the Bible for us tells me one thing: He wants to speak to us so we can know Him.

The culmination of God's speaking to us is the incarnation of Jesus Christ. The written Word of God points us to the living Word

---

[119] Ibid.
[120] Ibid.
[121] *Doctrine*, 44.

of God.[122] Some of my favorite verses in Scripture are Hebrews 1:1–3:

> Long ago, at many times and in many ways God spoke to our fathers by the prophets, but in these last days he has spoken to us by his Son, whom he appointed the heir of all things, though whom he also created the world. He is the radiance of the glory of God and the exact imprint of his nature, and he upholds the universe by the word of his power. After making purification for sins, he sat down at the right hand of the Majesty on high.

Jesus came in human flesh like you and me. He looked like us, He talked like us, He became hungry and tired like us. He had family and friends like we do. Yet Jesus lived without any sin and showed us what God the Father is like, being "the exact imprint of his nature." Jesus also died in our place for our sin so that we could have a relationship with God. The Father's ultimate Word to you is that He wants to be in a relationship with you so much that He sent his own Son to make that possible. God initiates the relationship: He speaks first, He pursues you, He's truthful and reliable and sacrificial. Quite the opposite of someone who lies, deceives, and distorts the truth in order to preserve or promote their own interests.

But surely God does not tell us all there is to know. God tells us, "For my thoughts are not your thoughts, neither are your ways my ways, declares the LORD. For as the heavens are higher than the earth, so are my ways higher than your ways, and my thoughts than your thoughts."[123] Our human, fallen minds cannot understand all of who God is or how He works. My pastor likes to say, "God is not only bigger than you think, He's bigger than you *can* think."

---

[122] From *Doctrine*
[123] Isaiah 55:8–9

But does this mean that He is holding back the whole truth? Is He deceiving us? This element of mystery might seem a little uncomfortable to you, especially if you had a dad who wasn't completely truthful. But think about it this way. My kids don't ask to see the family budget, how much money comes in, what the bills are, how much money there is for food or other needs. They just trust that Daddy and Mommy love them and will take care of them. They don't need to know all the details. In fact, knowing all the details of our finances would surely overwhelm them. We don't lie to our kids; we don't deceive them or purposefully hold back information from them, but we are completely truthful in a way that they can understand. God is a Father like that. If I knew all of the things that were going to occur in my life, I'm sure I'd be overwhelmed to the point of paralysis. Quite frankly, I don't want to know everything. I'd rather trust my Father who does.

Relationship, not Rules

The whole point of God speaking to you is that He wants a relationship with you—a relationship that is close, warm, loving, and secure; a relationship based on truth and not even a hint of a lie. Romans 10:17 says, "So then faith comes by hearing, and hearing through the word of God." In speaking to us, God wants us to know about Him and His love for us so that we'll love and trust Him in return. Too many people think the Bible is a book of rules we need to follow in order to be a "good person." The Bible does tell us how to live so that we'll please God and experience His blessing.[124] But studying the Bible and doing what it says isn't primarily about ticking off boxes; it's about living in relationship with our Father who made the world and knows how life works best.

The Bible is also not a self-help book. We can't just flip to the concordance in the back and see what the Bible has to say about finances, marriage, or making life decisions like it is a handbook with

---

[124] See Deuteronomy 12:28.

formulaic answers. The word of God is living and active,[125] and the Holy Spirit dwelling in us illuminates Scripture for us, showing us how to apply it to our hearts and lives. Through reading God's word, we learn about who He is, how He feels about us, and how to live an abundant and healthy life. It's like the conversations I overhear at night when my husband is putting our daughters to bed. They read a passage of the Bible and talk about what it means. What does it tell us about God? What does it tell us about ourselves? How can we be more like Jesus? How can we show God's love to others? God is a Father like that. He wants to communicate with you in order to have a relationship with you so that you become closer to Him and more like His Son.

As I previously said, Jesus is the ultimate expression of God desiring to connect with us. Jesus is God's Word in the flesh, who came to lay down his own life so that we could be in a relationship with God. This is unique in all religions and spiritualities. Every other belief system on earth tells people that they need to work, perform, or achieve a certain status in order to reach up to their god. Only our God comes down to bring His Word, His love, and Himself to us. Because of this, we can trust God's motives. There is nothing that we have done to deserve His pursuit of us. There is nothing we could ever do in our own power to attain the perfection that is His. Instead, Jesus the Living Word came to bridge the gap for us. The point of God's speaking to us is that we are invited into a close, secure, loving relationship with Him that will endure for all time.

So if God is incapable of saying anything that is untrue, then everything He says about Himself is true. But here's the kicker: what He says about *you* is true too.

> He says that He knit you together in your mother's womb (Ps.139:13).

> He says that when you know his truth, it will set you free (John 8:32).

---

[125] Hebrews 4:12

He says that you can be forgiven in Christ (1 John 1:9).

He says that there is no condemnation for you when you belong in Christ Jesus (Rom. 8:1).

He says that your sins were once a scarlet, and he can make them white as snow (Isa.1:18).

He says that in Christ you are a new person (2 Cor. 5:17).

He says that nothing can separate you from His love (Rom. 8:38–39).

He says that He will write His Word on your heart (Jer. 31:33).

He says if you belong to Him, you will someday see Him face-to-face (1 Cor. 13:12).

He says He will wipe away every tear from your eyes (Rev. 21:4).

He says someday everything will be good, new, and right (Rev. 21:5).

We can be reminded of these truths every time we open the Bible. Hearing from God every day though His word is how our soul receives nourishment. Just as our physical bodies need good quality food to thrive, so, too, does our soul need the spiritual food of the Bible to be healthy. I encourage you to spend time every day in God's Word. It doesn't have to be a complicated or lengthy study. What I've learned is that consistency matters more than anything. You can simply start with the verses I've listed above. I would suggest writing them out, praying over them, and meditating on them, and be prepared for God to make them come alive in your heart and teach you something you never knew before. God your Father wants to speak to you and be in relationship with you. He always tells the truth. You never need to question His motives or if He's deceiving you. You can believe everything He says, including what He says about you.

Heavenly Father,
I praise you as the source of all truth.
I am so grateful that there is not a shred of falsehood,
deception, or distortion in you.
Thank you for speaking to me in a way that I can understand,
and for sending Jesus to be the embodiment of all that You are.
I pray that your Spirit would create in me
a renewed love for your Word.
In Jesus's name,
amen.

11

My Heavenly Father Never Changes

My dad was unpredictable.

The first thing that caught my eye when I met my husband was his steadiness. Okay, that was actually the second thing. The first thing was his tall, bearded, cowboy-shirt-wearing good looks. But it's true that my husband is as steady as they come. We've never had a yelling match in our marriage, though we have had disagreements (we're human). In fact, in eleven years together, I've never heard him raise his voice in anger to anyone. Brandon is allergic to drama. He stays very calm even in tough situations and conversations. Brandon's reactions to situations fit their size; he doesn't get irrationally upset about things that are small. Brandon is also emotionally mature in that he handles his own thoughts and feelings in an adult manner. He doesn't "leak" negative emotions onto others who aren't involved in the situation but rather seeks out a wise and trusted friend to confide in. Ultimately, Brandon's faith in God's goodness and provision is the foundation for his life, and it shows in his steadiness.

Maybe Brandon's steadiness is due to the way God made him, but I think it's also a result of how he was raised. His dad, Steve, is the same way—as steady as they come. Brandon never questioned his dad's love, devotion, and commitment to the family. He confidently believed that everything his dad did was to bless the family. His dad was the "backstop" that he needed in life—the one he could go to for wisdom, encouragement, instruction, and help.

Brandon's steadiness has also helped him to be a great dad. However, he would say that, being full-blooded Norwegian, he can be a bit "emotionally constipated." Expressing emotions doesn't come naturally to him. That blessed "steadiness" can be taken too far. Perhaps that is why God gave us three daughters in a row. (Baby number four was a boy.) In the years since we've had children, God has grown Brandon in becoming more tender, affectionate, and better at expressing emotions without becoming overly emotional. Even though he's grown in tenderness, he's never lost that steadiness. Our children know what they're going to get with their dad. If they disobey, they'll probably receive consequences and discipline but never anger or punishment. If they are struggling or get hurt, Daddy will give them compassion and help. He never snaps in anger or frustration or pulls away from them in disappointment.

Our kids also know that Daddy is always up for a good time. When the kids want to go to the park, Daddy creates fun games and obstacle courses. When they want to swim in the pool, Daddy cannonballs off the rock wall, making huge waves that splash over the sides. He's better than I am at all of these things. (I can't say he's a better parent than me in all areas because if it weren't for me, the kids would probably be naked and starving. Or more likely, they'd have on dirty clothes and eat nachos for most meals). To my kids, Daddy is safe, loving, kind, fun, forgiving, and faithful. Daddy brings strength, safety, and stability to our home, our family, and indeed all of life. What kid wouldn't want a dad like that?

Unfortunately, some of us grew up with dads who were the opposite of steady. They were unpredictable. The Cambridge dictionary defines *unpredictable* as "tending to change suddenly and without reason or warning, and therefore not able to be depended upon."[126] The result of such unpredictability is that we aren't sure who Dad is or how he feels about us. Did your dad's moods vary wildly, and sometimes you didn't even know the reason why? Did

---

[126] https://dictionary.cambridge.org/us/dictionary/english/unpredictable

your dad tend to spend time with you when it was convenient for him but not always when you needed it most? Did your dad sometimes overreact to small instances of disobedience? Did the punishment not fit the crime, so to speak? Or perhaps your dad drank, and when he'd had too much, he became volatile or even violent. When your dad was stressed about work or finances, did you have to walk on eggshells to not set him off?

To be fair, if these things describe your dad in any way, he probably has (or had) some unhealed hurt of his own. Whereas women are much more prone to recognize and talk about their feelings and struggles, men oftentimes appear angry, aggressive, or erratic instead of sad. Recognizing that your dad probably had his own pain can give you more perspective, compassion, and help you to forgive him.

While it's important to realize that our dads are people too, the fact remains that when your dad cannot be trusted or relied upon, you don't feel loved, you don't feel secure, and you probably guard yourself from his erratic behavior. Your relationship can't grow or thrive in that kind of environment. Instead there is usually distance and even sometimes division in the relationship. Usually, a small child is attached to mom for the first few years of life. Dad is thus usually a child's first link to the outside world. So if your dad is unpredictable, you won't be sure who he is or how he feels about you. If that's the case, you won't be sure of other things either—namely, your own identity, other relationships, the world around you, and God Himself.

An unpredictable dad can contribute to our belief that God the Father is capricious, unreliable, and frightening. This is a key reason why some of us are more comfortable with Jesus and the New Testament than we are with the Father and the Old Testament. I've heard people say, "Well, I'm okay with Jesus, but I don't know about that angry guy in the Old Testament." The truth is that God the Father is a dad like my husband—safe, loving, kind, fun, forgiving, and faithful—only infinitely better.

God's Immutable Nature

In Exodus 3, Moses was tending his flocks in the wilderness when God appeared to him in a burning bush. God said that He had seen what his children, the people of Israel, had suffered under the Egyptians and He had come down to deliver them.[127] God chose to use Moses to bring them out of captivity. Moses was nervous and asked God, "Who should I say sent me?" God told Moses, "I AM WHO I AM... Say this to the people of Israel, 'I AM has sent me to you.'" Some translations say, "I will be who I will be." The theological word for this attribute of God is that He is *immutable*, meaning that He doesn't change. God is the only being in the whole universe who was not created; this makes Him completely unique to anything or anyone else in the universe. He is the sole Creator; everything else was created—people, angels, planets, stars, atoms, plants, animals, viruses, the mountains, the seas, and on and on. Only God has no beginning and no end.[128]

God is also One.[129] Though God is One God in three persons, which we call the Trinity, He is One in essence and nature. This is a mystery too deep for our tiny human brains to comprehend, but it is essential to who God is. There are no parts in God that could shift, move, or cause any type of alteration in his being. In addition, no outside thing can enter into God's being and cause a change.[130] God is also perfect; there are no flaws in Him, no faults, no need to grow or develop. The bottom line is that who God is right now is who He's always been and who He always will be. He is *immutable*.

Jesus used this same phrase "I am" to describe himself. In John 8, the Pharisees were engaged in a long argument with Jesus about his identity. The back-and-forth exchange culminates like this. Jesus says, "You claim that you know the Father, but you don't love me, and I come from Him."[131] Furthermore, the Pharisees claimed that Abraham was their spiritual father. Again, Jesus pointed out the hol-

---

[127] Exodus 3:14
[128] See Hebrews 1:12, Revelation 1:8.
[129] Deuteronomy 6:4
[130] Tozer, A.W. *The Knowledge of the Holy*, 77.
[131] See John 8:41–42

lowness of their assertion. "Your father Abraham rejoiced that he would see my day. He saw it and was glad… Truly, truly, I say to you, before Abraham was, I am." In saying this phrase "I am," Jesus was not only claiming to be greater than both Abraham and the prophets, he was also claiming to be the One true immutable God. We know this because the Pharisees "picked up stones to throw at him, but Jesus hid himself and went out of the temple."[132] They raged at Jesus's answer because they believed it to be blasphemy. Jesus got away this time, but they would ultimately crucify him for, as they said, being a mere man who claimed to be God.[133] The Pharisees wanted to take the Father but not Jesus; many people in our day are okay with Jesus but not the Father. However, from the Old Testament through to the New Testament, God is consistent in his claim to be One immutable God.

The Father's Immutable Affections

God's immutable nature means that his affections toward us are immutable as well.[134] While we may be familiar with God's describing himself as "I AM," oftentimes we don't realize that He expresses it with his Father's heart. In Exodus 3, He told Moses He was coming to rescue His children out of Egyptian captivity.[135] He was a Dad who saw His kids in distress and was determined to rescue them and bring them into a land of freedom and a life of fruitfulness.[136]

The Father did this again when He sent Jesus to earth as Immanuel, God with us. The Father didn't rescue us from Satan, sin, and death with his power and might as He did in Exodus when He sent the plagues upon Egypt and rescued Israel. No, this time, God the Father sent Jesus to earth to live like us as our Big Brother and to die in our place for our sin, thereby conquering Satan, sin, and death and putting them to open shame.[137]

---

[132] John 8:59
[133] .John 10:33
[134] Tozer, A.W. *The Knowledge of the Holy*, 82.
[135] Exodus 3:10
[136] Exodus 3:8
[137] Colossians 2:15

For God [the Father] so loved the world,
that he gave his only Son, that whoever believes
in him should not perish but have eternal life.[138]

You need to know that God isn't a distant being who is merely saying, "I am the creator of all things, I am self-existent, and I never change, so obey me." Rather God is our loving Father who says, "I never change. I have always and will always love you. So you can feel safe with me, and you can trust me, even when you fail and fall. I sacrificed my own Son so that we could be together." There is a vast difference between an impersonal divine force/ruler/being and a personal Father God. If you're being completely honest, which one do you believe God is? I once heard a pastor say that we can only get as close to God as our concept of Him will allow. You will not be close to God if you believe Him to be an impersonal force or faraway ruler. You will only be close to Him when you believe that He is your Father.

The book of Malachi gives us another good illustration of God's immutable, Fatherly affections toward his children. As the final book of the Old Testament, this is God's final word to his children before four hundred years of silence, followed by the most important event in all of human history: the birth of Jesus Christ. So this little book is big in its importance. The book of Malachi is essentially God calling a family meeting. He's a Dad who deeply loves his kids, but they've strayed from Him, and as a result they're not healthy. Instead they're disobeying Him, dishonoring Him, and destroying themselves. In Malachi 3:6, God says, "For I the LORD do not change." For a long time, the people of Israel had not been obeying God, yet he didn't change. Neither did he change his position and identity as Father God nor did he change his affections toward them. He says to his people, "Return to me, and I will return to you."[139] God did allow Israel to experience many consequences of their severe disobedience (God's people were conquered and enslaved by other godless nations for hundreds of years). God could also have wiped them out

---

[138] John 3:16
[139] Malachi 3:7

118

and been justified in doing so. But He didn't because they were his children and what He wanted more than anything was a relationship with them. God asks them—once again—to obey Him, "And thereby put me to the test, says the LORD of hosts, if I will not open the windows of heaven for you and pour down for you a blessing until there is no more need."[140] This doesn't necessarily mean that if we obey God, He will open the floodgates of heaven and we'll be "healthy, wealthy, and wise." But the principle we can learn from this scenario is that God is a good Dad who doesn't change his standards or His ways. He will not bless disobedience because it is harmful to us. God doesn't change His affections for us either. In fact, He asks for our obedience *because* He loves us. The Father wants us to live our lives in relationship with Him, walking in His ways, and receiving His blessing. God's way is *the* way to the happiest, healthiest, holiest life imaginable.

What God's Immutability Means for You

A. W. Tozer says, "His attitude toward us now is the same as it was in eternity past and will be in eternity to come."[141] This is such comfort in a world where people often change how they think, feel, and act toward us, sometimes depending on their personal interests and sometimes for the slightest reason.

Your Father is always on duty. He's never too busy to listen to you whether your cares are big or small. He's always receptive, and He'll always respond in love, mercy, and faithfulness. His will is to always love you, always be in relationship with you, and to have you lead a healthy and fruitful life. Whereas most relationships go through cycles of affection, ups and downs, your Father's affections and enthusiasm for you never wane.

Your Father's attitude toward sin is always the same. He hates it as a mother hates the sickness that is ravaging her child. Yet His

---

[140] Malachi 3:10

[141] Tozer, *The Knowledge of the Holy*, 72. Much in these closing paragraphs is adapted from Chapter 9 "The Immutabilty of God."

attitude toward the sinner is always the same too. Your Father's hands are extended in an open invitation for forgiveness, love, and relationship.

While God's immutability and perfection mean that we will always be the ones who need to make changes, it is always for the better. It is always for our good. While change is a bad thing in the fallen world (sin leads to death, creation is under the curse), it is a good thing for the child of God. Because we can change, we can be redeemed. We can be transformed and made new. So for the child of God the Father, change means the liar can become truthful; the promiscuous can become pure' the weak can become strong; the proud can become humble. The immutable God can transform our thoughts, desires, and affections by bringing us into a close, loving, secure relationship with Himself.

In Him, we can find the permanence that everyone in the history of the world has ever longed for. Tozer says, "Chance and change are busying our little world of nature and men, but in Thee we find no variableness nor shadow of turning. We rest in Thee without fear or doubt and face our tomorrows without anxiety."[142] Your mind can be renewed. Your soul can find forgiveness and rest. Your heart can find healing. Your Father won't change. And neither will His love for you.

Heavenly Father,
I praise you for your immutability.
I cannot fathom that you have never and will never change,
but I pray that you would help me to believe it.
Help me to also believe that your affections
toward me will never change.
I pray that when I am old and gray,
I would testify to coming generations
that you indeed are unchanging in your love and faithfulness.
In Jesus's name,
amen.

---

[142] Tozer, *The Knowledge of the Holy*, 75.

12

My Heavenly Father's Love Is a Gift

My dad made me earn his love.

"I was a pastor's daughter, you know, so I wasn't allowed to do that." This lovely woman in her late eighties had a faraway look in her eye, remembering her girlhood dream of being on her school's cheerleading squad. She wasn't allowed to, however, because she grew up in the 1940s when it would have been improper for a "pastor's daughter" to do such a thing. She continued to list the many things she was expected to do—dress modestly, get good grades in school, serve at church, always be on her best behavior—as well as the things she was not allowed to do—date boys, go to high school parties, or listen to rock 'n' roll. Essentially, she was expected to be perfect. It was a lot to live up to. Too much obviously since she remembers the weight of it all these years later.

Can you relate to this woman? Maybe your dad expected you to continue in the family business or to be a doctor or lawyer or businesswoman. Maybe you feel like you don't measure up to his standards because you're not married or don't have children. Or perhaps your dad's expectations are smaller but still mandatory in his eyes: you don't come to all the family holidays; you don't call home often enough; you're not grateful enough for what he provided for you. The result of a father-daughter dynamic like this is that you're always trying to live up to his expectations. If you achieve

_____, you'll earn your dad's pleasure and affection. How would you fill in the blank? The problem is that dads who operate like this usually keep moving the goalposts, continually making you achieve something or behave a certain way in order to earn their love and approval. Maybe you're a type-A superstar and you're able to make that happen most of the time, but you're exhausted and afraid to let up. Maybe your relationship is like a roller coaster—some days you do well in pleasing your dad, but other days you disappoint him. That's also exhausting. Maybe your dad's expectations were far too high, so you didn't even try to achieve them, and you're left feeling like a failure. The result of all of these potential outcomes is that you feel like you're not enough for your dad.

Once for All Time

The root problem is that this describes a transaction, not a relationship. In this type of situation, I get compensation for what I give, whether it's a little or a lot, whether it's acceptable or not. So if I do well, I get love. If I don't do well, I don't get love. I definitely don't get compassion for when I need help, fail, struggle, or need encouragement. This is a straightforward transaction. I get what I pay for. If I pay a lot, I get a lot. If I pay a little, I only get a little.

This dynamic does damage beyond your relationship with your dad because it also distorts how you view God the Father. God, being holy and perfect Himself, demands perfection from us if we are to be in a relationship with him. This much is true. But a dad who makes us earn his love leads us to believe that God does the same. So when we fall short of God's requirement for perfection, we can believe he's upset, disappointed, and possibly even angry with us. In short, we can wrongly believe that God demands our perfection but doesn't show compassion for our weakness. We don't feel close to God and are always trying to do better in our own power.

This is one of those times in which many of us know what is correct in our minds—that God loves us more than we'll ever know and that nothing we do or don't do will never change that. Yet in our lives, we don't emotionally feel that way, and so we don't live that way.

Yes, God demands perfection from us if we are to be in close relationship with him. Jesus himself said, "You therefore must be perfect, as your heavenly Father is perfect."[143] Yet God knows your limitations. He knows that you could give all your energy for every minute of every day for all eternity, and you'd never be able to remotely come close to the life of sinless obedience necessary to get back into close relationship with him. So God, your loving Father, provided His only Son Jesus as substitute for what you'd have to spend eternity to even attempt to earn. Jesus paid your debt of sin that you could never hope to repay. Hebrews 10:12 says, "But when Christ had offered *for all time a single sacrifice for sins*, he sat down at the right hand of God" (emphasis mine). Do you see that? Christ died for your sin, my sin, and the sin of every person who has ever and will ever live. And then He sat down, which is to say "It is finished." If you've spent any time in church, I know you've probably heard this countless times, but I want you to feel it in your soul. I pray that the Holy Spirit would remove any weight or obligation of performance that you may feel.

There is no payment left for your sin. There is nothing left for you to do, achieve, earn, or contribute that will make you pleasing in the sight of your Father. There is nothing you need to do to earn His love or earn a relationship with Him. There is no transaction left for you to conduct because Jesus conducted the one and only transaction that was necessary. Your debt is paid in full. You are forgiven in Christ. Indeed, "Where there is forgiveness of these (sins), there is no longer any offering for sin."[144] Once for all time. It is finished.

I have been in churches where the gospel was taught in this "transactional" way. Christ died to take away your sin and to give you his righteousness. Jesus did in fact perform what some theologians call "the great exchange." But the transaction is now done and what's left is for you to be in relationship with your Father. It is good for

---

[143] Matthew 5:48
[144] Hebrews 10:18

123

us to realize and appreciate the gravity of what Jesus suffered on our behalf. Jesus himself said that when we are forgiven of much, we love much. But some churches do people a disservice when they focus exclusively on feeling the weight of Jesus taking the punishment for our sin and fail to move on to growing close to God in relationship. The result is that people can end up getting stuck in this transactional thinking. I've also heard some Bible teachers say that our life should now be one of grateful obedience for what Jesus has done for us. To me, this almost sounds like I need to "pay God back" for sending Jesus to take my place. This kind of teaching makes life in relationship with the Father seem like a "have to" when it should be a "get to." We should feel deeply grateful, and we should do what God asks us to do, but we definitely don't need to pay God back. There is no vengeance in the Father. He doesn't keep a record of our sins. He does not keep score. Jesus's death, burial, and resurrection in your place wiped out the scorecard. Your Father sent Jesus as a free gift.

Think about it. When you give someone a birthday gift, do you expect any sort of payment in return? A true, grateful, heartfelt "thank you" is appreciated. But you don't want the person to hand you a $20 bill to help chip in for their birthday gift. You don't want them to thank you profusely every day for the rest of their life for the gift. You gave them a gift because you love them, that's it. There was no exchange of money or other compensation. God is the great Giver who gave Jesus out of His overflowing love for you. Hear me on this: the Father's motivation for sending Jesus to die in your place was and is His love for you and His desire to be in relationship with you. He forgives sin, brings you close, changes you, and makes you more like Jesus because He loves you and that's what's best for you. Yes, we ought to obey him, but out of love and trust that His way is the best way and because we want to be close to our Father. God doesn't need anything from you. He literally created the universe with just a few verbal commands. There's nothing that you could offer to God that He needs. Jesus performed the one and only transaction that was necessary. What the Father wants from you is a relationship.

In Luke 15, Jesus tells the well-known parable of the prodigal son. Except, we are going to focus on the father in the story, who is supposed to show us what God the Father is like. It's important to know that Jesus told this parable as the last one in a series of three. In each of the three parables, we see someone searching for something that is lost, finding it, and then rejoicing! Luke begins chapter 15 by telling us, "Now the tax collectors and sinners were all drawing near to hear him. And the Pharisees and the scribes grumbled, saying, 'This man receives sinners and eats with them.[145]'" The religious leaders were incensed that Jesus would befriend nasty "sinners." Jesus used all three parables to show the religious leaders that the Father's desire is to love, forgive, and accept sinners—people who had nothing to give Him in return. The religious leaders saw God's interaction with people in the transactional way, not the relational way. And Jesus corrects them.

If you are already familiar with the story of the prodigal son, I want you to look at it in a new way. The story begins with the younger son demanding that his father give him his inheritance. Since an inheritance is meant to be given once the father dies, this son was essentially saying that it would be better for him if his dad were dead. He wanted his dad's money, and he wanted independence, but he didn't want his dad. And that's exactly what he got. The dad gave the younger son his portion of the inheritance, which would have been one-third of the father's estate. The dad likely would have had to sell off some of his assets in order to give his younger son his share of the inheritance. See this scene in your mind's eye: the dad, who is still living and still needs to be able to provide for his household, handed over a sizable chunk of money to his foolish, rebellious teenage son. The son turned his back and left home, never looking over his shoulder, not saying goodbye. The dad stood there heartbroken, watching his son walk away, not knowing if he'd ever return.

Jesus continues the story, saying the son then went to a "far country, and there he squandered his property in reckless living."[146] Imagine a young man buying cars, clothes, and rounds of drinks for everyone he meets. Perhaps even drugs and prostitutes. Have you

---

[145] Luke 15:1–2
[146] Luke 15:13

ever seen a movie where there's someone flinging dollar bills into the crowd like they're playing cards? That was this kid. Just wanton, reckless spending. He was flying high—until his money was gone. He had nothing left when a famine struck the land. No family, no money, and all those new friends he thought he had made were no friends at all. Finally, he took the only job he could find. He fed pigs, which would have been considered unclean to all Jewish people. He was so destitute, so hungry and needy that "he was longing to be fed with the pods that the pigs ate."[147] Envision this young man's catastrophic decline. He began as a boisterous young man spending wildly on possessions and partying but collapsed into a skinny, sickly, smelly, scared young man ready to eat pig food. He had officially hit rock bottom. And he had no one to blame but himself. As a parent, the thought of something like this happening to one of my children makes my insides ache.

And then, in Luke 15:17 we find that the son "came to himself." Some translations say that "he finally came to his senses." He said, "How many of my father's hired servants have more than enough bread, but I perish here with hunger! I will arise and go to my Father, and I will say to him, 'Father, I have sinned against heaven and before you. I am no longer worthy to be called your son. Treat me as one of your hired servants.'"[148] The son finally stopped to consider what he was doing and where his life was headed, and he realized that his dad really is a good dad. He ran away from his dad's presence but not his love. In true humility and repentance for his rebellious ways, the son turned around and headed home.

Can you imagine what the dad went through while his son was away? He looked for him every day, asking other people if they had heard from him or had news of how he was doing. Every day the son was gone, the dad must have been sick with worry, perhaps trying to accept that he might never see his son again. But one day, as the dad peered down the road, there he was! Could it be true? Yes, his son was coming up the road! The Bible says, "But while he [the son] was

---

[147] Luke 15:16
[148] Luke 15:17–19, emphasis mine

still a long way off, the father *felt compassion*, and ran and embraced him and kissed him." A grown man hiking up his robes and running was not seen as dignified in that culture. But the dad didn't care! His son was home! The son had barely uttered his apology and the dad cut him off, shouting, "Let's have a party! Get my son the best clothes, get him cleaned up, prepare the best food we have, put on some music! We're celebrating!" Can you see it? The dad and the son are embracing, laughing, crying tears of joy and relief. The mother, the servants, the entire household is running to greet the son and shower him with love. Their prayers had been answered! He was lost but now he's home!

Culturally and legally speaking, the dad could have disowned his son, the way his son had disowned him. The dad could have beaten him, berated him with words, or even had him killed. But the dad didn't do any of those things. In fact, he didn't even ask where the money went. He didn't ask why his son looked and smelled so awful. The dad didn't question where the son had been or what he had done. He didn't hire him as a servant or devise a repayment plan. In fact, he spent even more money on his son by celebrating his return to the family. The father felt compassion for what his son had endured and desired for a relationship going forward. It did not matter how much money the son had wasted nor how much it cost to celebrate his homecoming. All the father cared about was that the son he had lost was now found. This is not a transaction; this is grace.

Remember, God the Father sent Jesus to earth to conduct the only transaction that was necessary. Jesus paid the price for your sin on the cross and now offers you forgiveness and eternal life as a free gift. It doesn't matter what you've done, where you've been, where you have failed or fallen down. Because of Jesus, your Father doesn't keep score, weighing your good deeds against your bad ones. He doesn't want you to run yourself ragged trying to earn a love He freely lavishes on you as a gift of grace. He just wants you to come to Him and lose yourself in his loving embrace. He just wants you to come home.

Heavenly Father,
I confess that sometimes I feel that I need to earn your love.
But I know that you sent Jesus
to live the life of obedience that I cannot,
and to die the death for sin that I should die.
I thank you that you see me clothed in Christ,
and that this is a gift that I don't need to repay.
I pray the Holy Spirit would help me to feel your love,
your healing, and your acceptance of me as your daughter.
In Jesus's name,
amen.

13

My Heavenly Father Forgives Me Completely

My dad won't forgive me.

Jane's relationship with her dad had been quite rocky for several years following her parents' divorce. Each conversation was similar—him bringing up the past, telling her why he had done nothing wrong, justifying his actions, and insisting Jane was the one who needed to change. It felt like running on a hamster wheel. They were having the same conversation over and over again without making any progress. But finally, during one such conversation, the Holy Spirit showed Jane what was actually going on. She now realized that her dad hadn't forgiven her for some things she had done but was instead harboring bitterness. In addition, if there could be any future for the relationship, she was expected to do what he wanted. There was no back and forth in their conversations or their actions; no give and take, so to speak. Jane was supposed to give so her dad could take. It was his way or the highway. Jane's dad said that he was a Christian, so this confused her. What about what God wanted? What about doing what was right in His eyes? What about forgiveness?

Jane admits that she did need to apologize for some of the things she had done and said to her dad. She was under no delusions that she was perfect. Many times over the years, especially in those first tumultuous years following her parents' divorce, Jane had said some things she regretted, as people often do when emotions are running high. Despite apologizing for these things, her dad was not satisfied. Instead of talking to Jane directly, her dad would often involve other family members by leaking his feelings of displeasure onto them. Jane's dad also brought up things from the past over and over again, even when she thought she had apologized for them. He portrayed himself as a victim and Jane as a bad daughter who had said and done hurtful things to him. Jane didn't know what to do with a dad who acted like he was perfect and would never apologize for things he had done yet demanded that she repent of anything that displeased him, hurt his feelings, or made him look bad. Even if she did what he wanted her to, would he ever be truly satisfied? Would he ever truly forgive her? Jane was confused. What was she supposed to do with a dad who, essentially, tried to sit on God's throne and act as her judge? What was she supposed to do with a dad who kept a list of all her wrongdoings and wouldn't let them go?

Can you relate to any of these things that Jane was feeling about her unforgiving dad? If so, maybe you struggle, like Jane did, to believe that God the Father is not the same way. What we say we believe and how we actually live our lives often don't match up. We may know in our head that Jesus atoned for our sin on the cross, but if we are projecting the character of our unforgiving dad onto our forgiving Father, we may not actually believe it in our hearts. Jane would have said that the Father had forgiven her sin because of Jesus's work on the cross, but deep down, she still wondered if He kept a record of her wrongs. Jane often asked herself, "Did I feel bad enough for my sin? Did I really mean it when I told God I was sorry and asked for forgiveness? I messed up again, so maybe He didn't forgive me and I need to start all over." Like Jane, we can question if we're really forgiven, if God is upset with us, and if he's keeping a list of our wrongs like our dad did.

A Picture of God's Forgiveness

As we discussed in the previous chapter, God the Father doesn't keep record of our sin because of what Jesus has done for us. Jesus paid the price for our sin in full. He wiped our debt to the Father clean, a debt we could never hope to repay ourselves. In the greatest exchange in the history of the world, Jesus took our sin and gave us his righteousness. God is a loving Father who provided Jesus as a substitute for us so that we wouldn't have to die for our sin but could instead have eternal life with Him. The Father took it upon himself to remove any and every obstacle of sin that stood between you and Him. "But God shows his love for us in that while we were still sinners, Christ died for us."[149] That is forgiveness. Our debt was canceled not by our own doing but by His.

While we usually look to the cross to remember God's forgiveness for us (and rightfully so), there is another picture of the Father's forgiveness in the Old Testament that is helpful in deepening our understanding of what that forgiveness means. For this, we're going all the way back to Leviticus. Don't worry. I promise this will be much more interesting than it sounds!

In Leviticus 16, God introduced what would become the most important day of the year for the Israelites, the Day of Atonement. This annual ceremony was intended to cleanse the sin of the people so that it would no longer separate them from God and He could continue to dwell in their presence. We won't go through all of the details of this ceremony, but I want to look at one part in particular that is often overlooked by Christians in our day, even though it beautifully foreshadowed Jesus's work on the cross. The high priest would select two young goats that were healthy and without blemish, representing sinless perfection. One goat was a sin offering. Though the people deserved to die for their sins, the high priest would slaughter the goat of the sin offering as a substitute in their place. Imagine that for a moment. What would it have been like to see blood spill forth from a young, pure animal and realize that that should be you? While we don't have bloody ceremonies anymore, the Israelites had them all the time and were constantly reminded of the seriousness of sin. In his book *Death by Love*, Mark Driscoll explains, "The goat was no longer innocent when it took the guilt of sin; it was a sin offering for the people (Lev. 16:15). Subsequently, its blood represented

---

[149] Romans 5:8

life given as payment for sin."[150] The high priest would then use the blood to cleanse the mercy seat on the ark of the covenant inside the most holy place in the tabernacle, as this was the place where God's presence would dwell. With the payment for sin satisfied, God could continue to dwell with his people.

The second goat was not killed. Rather, the high priest would lay his hands on the head of the goat and confess all the sins of the people. Think about how long this would take. The high priest had to confess *all* the sins people had committed since the ceremony was performed the previous year. This confession would symbolically transfer the sins of the people onto the goat. It was then sent away into the wilderness, taking all of the sin with it. This goat was called the scapegoat. Again, this was a very tangible way for people to see that God removes their sin from them. Think about putting your hands on the scapegoat. What sin still plagues you even though you've tried to stop countless times? What in your past or present are you ashamed that you've done? Is there anything your dad is still holding against you even though you have apologized and tried to make amends? What sin would you like to have carried off into the wilderness, never to be seen again?

Ultimately, the purpose of the Day of Atonement was to point to Jesus. Just as the first goat that was slaughtered in order to cleanse the tabernacle, Jesus was the ultimate unblemished sacrifice who shed his blood to cleanse us. "He entered once for all into the holy places, not by means of the blood of goats and calves but by means of his own blood, thus securing eternal redemption... For Christ has entered, not into holy places made with hands, which are copies of the true things, but into heaven itself, now to appear in the presence of God on our behalf."[151] There is no more sin standing between you and God because of the perfect, once-for-all-time sacrifice of Jesus Christ in your place. This is the essence of forgiveness. Instead of making you bear the penalty for your sin, God bore it instead.

---

[150] Driscoll, Mark. *Death by Love*, 21.
[151] Hebrews 9:12, 24

We also see a foreshadowing of Jesus in the role of the scape-goat. Just as the goat ran off into the wilderness, removing the sin of the people, so, too, did Jesus bear our sin on the cross and remove it from us.[152] Scripture tells us in many places that because of Jesus, God will remember our sin no more. What this means is that He will no longer hold our sin against us. Here are some key passages:

> I, yes I, am He who blots out your trans-gressions for My own sake and remembers your sins no more. (Isa. 43:25)

> No longer will each man teach his neighbor or his brother, saying, "Know the LORD," because they will all know Me, from the least of them to the greatest, declares the LORD. For I will forgive their iniquity and will remember their sins no more. (Jer. 31:34)

> He will again have compassion on us; He will vanquish our iniquities. You will cast out all our sins into the depths of the sea. (Micah 7:19)

> Their sins and lawless acts I will remember no more. (Heb. 10:17)

Your heavenly Father sent your Big Brother Jesus to not only pay the penalty for your sin but also to remove it so that before Him, you are clean. God your heavenly Father doesn't keep a record of your wrongs. Instead, He sent Jesus to take them away and wrap you up in his righteousness. There is nothing between you and your Father when you trust in Jesus's work on the cross in your place. *Your* debt of sin has been canceled by *Him* because He loves you and desires a relationship with you. This is ultimate forgiveness.

---

[152] Isaiah 53:11

Forgiven People Should Be Forgiving People

Because we have received the gift of forgiveness from God, Scripture tells us to extend forgiveness as a gift to others. Ephesians 4:31–32 (NIV) says, "Get rid of all bitterness, rage and anger, brawling and slander, along with every form of malice. Be kind and compassionate to one another, forgiving each other, just as Christ in God forgave you." As children of God, Christians are *forgiven* people and so ought to be *forgiving* people. Forgiveness isn't found anywhere else but from God through the work of Jesus Christ. Just take a look at the world around us. It is not uncommon for someone's life and career to be ruined when something unsavory from their past is dragged into the present and posted online for the world to see, no matter if the person has apologized or changed their ways. The world is a very unforgiving place. So by contrast, forgiving someone is one of the major ways we can share God's love with them.

I think a major factor in our struggle to forgive, especially people who are close to us that have wronged us, is that we don't clearly understand what biblical forgiveness looks like. Let's discuss seven myths about forgiveness and uncover the truth[153].

MYTH: It's not a big deal if I carry hurts and don't forgive people who have wronged me.
TRUTH: Forgiveness is a matter of spiritual warfare.

The absolute first and crucial thing to understand about forgiveness is that it is a matter of spiritual warfare. As we've just discussed, forgiveness is God's idea and only comes to us through the work of Jesus on the cross on our behalf. Unforgiveness, by contrast, comes directly from the enemy. "Satan and demons are never forgiven for anything, and they in turn never forgive anyone else for anything. Unforgiveness is demonic. To refuse to forgive is to open oneself

---

[153] Much of the content for these myths/truths is adapted from *Spirit-Filled Jesus* by Mark Driscoll.

to the realm of demonic activity."[154] Satan is the one who doesn't forgive. Satan is the one who keeps picking up the same rock and throwing it at you over and over again. Satan is the one who attacks your identity as a forgiven child of God. Satan is the one who accuses you. Satan is the one who lies to you. Satan is the one who wants to destroy you and your relationships. However, he is the one who will one day be finally and fully destroyed. By harboring unforgiveness in your heart, you are leaving a door open in your life for Satan. Do you leave the doors of your home unlocked when you're away or sleeping at night? Of course not. You don't want some unwanted intruder on your property. Unforgiveness is the spiritual equivalent of leaving your doors unlocked and your windows flung open to the presence of the enemy. I don't say that to scare you. I say that to implore you to forgive your dad, even if he hasn't forgiven you.

Colossians 2:13–15 says,

> And you, who were dead in your trespasses and the uncircumcision of your flesh, God made alive together with him, having forgiven us all our trespasses, by canceling the record of debt that stood against us with its legal demands. This he set aside, nailing it to the cross. He disarmed the rulers and authorities and put them to open shame, by triumphing over them in him.

The power of the demonic, the power of unforgiveness, has been disarmed in your life by the death, burial, and resurrection of Jesus Christ. You are forgiven in Him. Furthermore, the indwelling, supernatural power of the Holy Spirit is the power in you to forgive your dad or whoever else you need to forgive in your life. It is not in our fallen human nature to forgive; you need the power of the Holy Spirit to work through you, but that's his job. He loves to empower you to do things that glorify God and bless you and others. Unforgiveness is demonic; forgiveness is supernatural. As my pastor

---

[154] Driscoll, Mark. *Spirit-Filled Jesus,* 193.

says, you have to choose if you are going to pull hell up into your life (unforgiveness) or pull heaven down into your life (forgiveness).

MYTH: I was wronged, so I have the right to be angry.
TRUTH: Unforgiveness chains me to the past; forgiveness will set me free.

Hebrews 12:15 says, "See to it that no one fails to obtain the grace of God; that no "root of bitterness" springs up and causes trouble, and by it many become defiled." *Bitterness* by definition is hanging onto anger or disappointment when you feel you have been treated unfairly. The Bible says that bitterness is a like a root from which a gigantic troublesome weed grows up in your life. Robert Morris uses a different illustration of unforgiveness and bitterness: "Holding unforgiveness in your heart is like drinking poison, in the hopes that it will hurt the other person. Unforgiveness does not hurt the other person—it hurts you!… Unforgiveness will cause you to live in torment."[155]

Remember Jane, who we talked about at the beginning of the chapter? She experienced the negative effects of unforgiveness first-hand. After hearing a sermon on forgiveness at church one Sunday, Jane felt the Holy Spirit urging her to forgive her dad. More out of anger than a humble desire to forgive, she had a conversation with God, trying to process all that she was feeling. "My dad has done so many things wrong, and he's never apologized. He doesn't see how hurtful he's been. Or maybe he does see but doesn't care. Maybe he'd rather save face, then repair our relationship. Yeah, I'm angry, but it feels good to be angry. I'm hurting!" God clearly impressed upon her spirit, "Your anger doesn't feel nearly as good as forgiveness will." Jane knew immediately in her heart that God was right; she needed to forgive her dad because through her anger, bitterness, and holding onto past hurts, she was actually hurting herself. She struggled to forgive other people, not just her dad. Jane also had trouble trusting people in her life for fear that they would harm her the way her dad did. She also felt an underlying level of uncertainty in her relation-

---

[155] Morris, Rober, *Dream to Destiny*, 168.

ship with God; her lack of understanding of forgiveness left her wondering if God really and truly forgave her and if He kept a scorecard of everything she had done wrong. Yet in that moment of revelation, Jane prayed and asked the Holy Spirit to empower her to begin to forgive her dad; she knew it was the right thing to do.

Unforgiveness chains us to bad experiences that happened in the past. We revisit them and replay them until they damage our present and negatively impact our choices for the future. Forgiving someone digs out that root of bitterness in your life and allows God's love to heal you and move you beyond the past and into a future of healing and freedom.

MYTH: I need to receive an apology before I can forgive.
TRUTH: Forgiveness does not require an apology.

There is a false teaching out there—not just in the world's culture but also unfortunately from some Christians—that you cannot or should not forgive someone unless they first repent to you and ask for forgiveness. First of all, this false teaching is often impractical. Sometimes people never apologize, either because they don't think they did anything wrong, they don't care how we feel, or they're just plain evil. Unfortunately, sometimes the person we need to forgive is unsafe so we don't want to see or talk to them. Sometimes the person we need to forgive is no longer living. The result of the false teaching that forgiveness first requires an apology is this: if the other person has not, cannot, or will not apologize, I am doomed to feel wronged, hurt, and victimized. Waiting for someone to apologize before you forgive them does nothing to them; it only hurts you. It keeps you bound by bitterness, which you'll recall, the Bible says is a root that springs up and causes all kinds of trouble.[156]

The other option is to forgive someone as a free and unearned gift. Just as your forgiveness for your sin was paid for by Jesus on his cross, so, too, was the sin of the person who wronged you. Forgiveness means that you choose to no longer hang onto the offense but rather

---

[156] Hebrews 12:15

trust that God will deal with the person in His perfect way and timing. God loves justice, and He will execute it perfectly in His own time.[157] Again, this is easier said than done, and it will require supernatural empowerment by the Holy Spirit, but it is most definitely possible.

MYTH: Forgiveness means I cannot *make* a record of wrongs.
TRUTH: Forgiveness means I cannot *keep* a record of wrongs.

In 1 Corinthians 13, the famous "love" chapter in the Bible, the apostle Paul says that love "keeps no record of wrongs." Oftentimes we act as if we have forgiven someone but instead have continued to let their offense bother us. As a pastor once told me, "We nurse it, rehearse it, and curse it." We replay the offense over and over in our minds and sometimes leak it to other people as well. This is what Paul meant by keeping a record of wrongs.

However, the Bible does not say that you cannot *make* a record of wrongs. In fact, doing just that is often quite helpful. I have known many people who have written out all of their thoughts, feelings, and fears in a journal and then destroyed it. Sometimes it can even be helpful to write a letter to the person who has offended you, detailing all of the things you wish you could say to them. This letter is NEVER sent to that person but rather destroyed. It can be quite helpful and symbolic to write one of these letters and then burn it. Essentially, a journal or letter of this kind allows you to fully and freely express yourself while keeping it between you and God. It is a safe and personal way to deal with deep emotions without having to censor the words you choose. You may make a record of wrongs. You just can't keep it. You need to forgive the other person, give their wrongs to God, and trust God with the rest.

MYTH: Forgiveness means I am letting the other person get away with wrongdoing.
TRUTH: Forgiveness can still hold the offender responsible for his actions.

---

[157] Isaiah 61:8

When we feel we've been treated wrongly, we want to right the wrong. But vengeance only succeeds in dragging us down to the level of the person who offended us. It throws gasoline on the fire already burning in the relationship. Forgiveness does not forget about justice but rather trusts that God will act in perfect justice on our behalf. You can forgive someone but still create boundaries. You don't have to continue to clean up their mess, and you don't have to act to please them. Forgiving someone does not mean that you allow them to mistreat, misuse, or misspeak about you. You can forgive but still not want to be in a close relationship with someone. You can, but you don't have to. You can forgive but still not trust someone. "Forgiveness is free, but trust is earned. Forgiveness is for all people; trust is for safe people."[158] You can forgive someone and still call the police if a crime has been committed. Rather than acting in vengeance, you are protecting others from future harm.

I love how my pastor puts this: "You need to remind yourself of this truth continually. When you forgive someone, you are not allowing them to get away with anything but you are allowing yourself to get away from everything. When you forgive, you leave the field of battle where all the bleeding is happening. You stop focusing on winning and begin to focus on living. Forgiving is how you start healing."[159]

Your forgiveness is not God's forgiveness. In forgiving someone, you are remembering that you do not sit in the seat of judgment. God does. And He will act in perfect justice. Over and over in the Psalms, the author laments that evildoers appear to be getting away with their deeds. However, in the end, God will bring justice. People who continually sin and refuse to repent to God are storing up wrath for themselves for the day when God executes his judgment.[160] He will not let anyone get away with their sin, unless they have trusted in the Lord Jesus Christ as the payment for their sin. Either Jesus paid for their sin or they will pay for their sin. Those are the only two options. Forgiveness does not mean you are letting an offender get away with evil.

---

[158] Driscoll, Mark. *Spirit-Filled Jesus*, 175.
[159] Ibid. 176
[160] Romans 2:5

MYTH: Forgiveness is a one-time event.
TRUTH: Forgiveness is an ongoing process.

The disciple Peter asked Jesus how many times he should forgive someone who sins against him. Jesus replied, "seventy times seven," by which He meant to forgive without keeping count.[161] In fact, forgiveness really ought to be a way of life. After we initially forgive someone, it can take time to process all of the hurt we feel, one layer at a time. Sometimes we learn more information that brings up our pain once again. Other times, people commit the same offense over and over again. Still other times, some unrelated person or situation will trigger a painful memory from the past. All of these situations are instances where we'll have to make the choice to forgive someone again.

MYTH: I can't forgive myself for things I've done.
TRUTH: Only God forgives.

I have often heard women say, "I know God forgives me, but I can't forgive myself." There is no other worthy substitute for the payment of your sin than Jesus. There is no higher authority than God the Father. I have a newsflash for you: you are not above God, and that is a good thing. If He says you are forgiven, you are forgiven! If that is hard for you to believe for some reason, pray and ask the Lord what that reason is. If you are feeling conviction over something specific, that is likely the Holy Spirit inviting you to repent. You can confess that specific sin to the Lord and receive His forgiveness right now.

Perhaps you feel a more general sense of condemnation. Oftentimes the source of that type of feeling is Satan. Perhaps it's lingering shame over something you've done in the past. Perhaps it's that you struggle to believe that you are God's beloved daughter. Perhaps the enemy is lying to you or accusing you of something that God has already forgiven you for. Don't settle for saying, "I can't forgive myself," and hanging onto whatever that offense is. That is a lie of the enemy. The only forgiveness you need is God's, and that

---

[161] ESV Study Bible note on Matthew 18:21–22.

is available to you as a gift through Jesus Christ. God's forgiveness counts for all of you and all of your life.

Your Father Loves to Forgive

No matter how you feel you have messed up, come to God! He already knows everything you've done and everything you will ever do. All of your sin—past, present, and future—is covered by the work of Jesus on the cross. You have nothing to prove. Jesus is your payment for sin, your source of forgiveness and eternal life, and your freedom to live as a new, cleansed, beloved daughter of your heavenly Father. As difficult as it may seem, God can help you to forgive your dad. It may take time and be a messy process, but I truly believe today is the day to begin that journey. Remember that it is the enemy who doesn't want you to feel forgiven and doesn't want you to forgive your dad. Don't let him get away with that. Now that you know that Satan traffics in unforgiveness, you can spot his schemes and turn to God. Do not believe the lie that your heavenly Father is like your unforgiving dad: He does not keep a record of your wrongs; He canceled the payment due for your sin by the blood of Jesus; and He offers free and unfettered forgiveness for you. Your Heavenly Father loves to forgive, and he'll help you to extend that to others as well.

> *Heavenly Father,*
> *Thank you that you are a forgiving God.*
> *I am overwhelmed at your grace*
> *when I think of all that you have forgiven me for*
> *and that you will continue to forgive me.*
> *I confess that it is hard to forgive my dad.*
> *It hurts that he won't forgive me.*
> *I pray that despite his actions,*
> *I would trust you to carry out justice*
> *and that your Spirit would lead me*
> *through the process of forgiving my dad.*
> *In Jesus's name,*
> *Amen.*

14

My Heavenly Father Tells Me Who I Am

My dad labeled me.

One of the saddest verses in all of scripture to me is Genesis 3:8, "And they (Adam and Eve) heard the sound of the LORD God walking in the garden in the cool of the day, and the man and his wife hid themselves from the presence of the LORD God among the trees of the garden." Adam and Eve used to live in the very presence of God, naked and without shame. Yet they now hid themselves in fear and humiliation. Why? This exchange between Adam and God gets to the root of the situation:

> But the LORD God called to the man and said to him, "Where are you?" And he said, "I heard the sound of you in the garden and *I was afraid, because I was naked, and I hid myself.*" He [God] said, "*Who told you* that you were naked?" (Gen. 3:9–11a, emphasis mine)

God had given life to Adam and Eve, declared that they were made in His image, placed them in a beautiful garden, and blessed them with His presence. There shouldn't have been anything else they needed or desired. Yet Satan crept into the garden in the form of a cunning snake and attacked them at the core of who they were.

142

He brought into question their identity as God's children whom He loved and enjoyed by suggesting that God was holding out on them, that He was being stingy with them. Satan tempted Adam and Eve to rebel against God, convincing them they could have a better life if they made their own rules. He told them they didn't need to obey God, and instead they could be their own gods. Adam and Eve soon painfully learned that Satan is a liar, for the only result of their sin was that their perfect relationship with God (and one another) was shattered. They no longer felt safe with God but feared Him instead. With that relationship broken, Adam and Eve no longer knew who they were.

Identity is the way we see ourselves; it's who we think we are. In his book *Spirit-Filled Jesus*, Mark Driscoll explains why identity is so important:

> Who you think you are determines what you do. Because of this, when Satan attacks, he starts by undermining your sense of identity. In the first attack on humans Adam and Eve were told that if they did something (partake of the forbidden fruit), they would then achieve their identity by becoming "like God." That, however, was a lie. God had already made them in his "likeness." They had already received an identity of being like God, but somehow got spiritual amnesia and forgot who they were.[162]

Adam and Eve allowed someone other than God to define their identity, and it was a disaster. It led them to forget that they belonged to God and were loved by Him, and it led them to sin.

The question God asks Adam—"Who told you who you are?"—is one that is crucial for us to ask ourselves as well. Many of us would say that we get our identity from God; we know we are his child, that we are saved in Christ, and that we are loved by God.

---

[162] Driscoll, Mark, *Spirit-Filled Jesus*, 70.

But many of us don't truly live out of this identity. Instead, we are plagued by doubts about our value and worth. We worry if we are pretty enough, thin enough, or successful enough. We expend much energy trying to please the people in our lives, even to the detriment of our own health and well-being. Some of us overcommit because we are afraid to tell others no and risk letting them down. Others of us portray a life online that doesn't match up with our real life in an effort to gain acceptance and affirmation. We are burdened by worry, anxiety, and hurry. Since who we think we are determines what we do, all of these efforts reveal that we don't truly trust who God says we are and how He feels about us. This is why I want you to think about the same question posed to Adam and Eve: who told you who you are?

I grew up going to church but experiencing Christianity as list of rules rather than a relationship with God. I learned that age-old "trinity" of so-called Christian obedience: Don't smoke, drink, or have sex. I didn't do any of those things throughout middle school or high school. Then I went off to college and I did *all* of those things. I became a stereotypical "party girl." After college I began attending a great Bible-teaching church where I developed a real love for God and began to grow in maturity. Even then I still felt as if I was a "party girl" trying to be a Christian. That's what the enemy wanted me to believe. Just like he deceived Adam and Eve, Satan deceived me. He wanted me to believe that because I had started down the wrong road, I had to continue that direction. He wanted me to believe that I had ruined my life and my identity to the extent that I wasn't worthy to be called loved, forgiven, or clean. That is a flat out a lie. Although it took years to realize, I finally came to believe the truth that I could shed the "party girl" label. I am not defined by what I have done or what has been done to me but only by what Jesus has done for me. Only He gets to say who I am. And the same goes for you too.

When Dad Labels Me

Because dads are supposed to show their children what God the Father is like, they have tremendous influence in communicating to their children their God-given identity. Dads have two choices: they can either reinforce lying labels from the enemy, or they can fight against those lies with the truth of who God says their daughters are. Did your dad give you any negative labels? If you're not sure, first think about what labels you'd give yourself. What about the secret labels you keep to yourself? The ones you don't say out loud. The ones you feel that you can't seem to shed. Do you feel you are

- unlovable?
- dirty?
- broken?
- too much of _____?
- not enough of _____?
- the "black sheep" of the family?
- a troublemaker?
- a failure?
- a disappointment?
- a hypocrite?
- hopeless?

Sadly, I could make a list as long as my arm of labels I've heard women give themselves. Even more tragically, some of these came from their dads, who were supposed to have shown them the love of the Father, making them feel accepted and secure. You might know in your mind that whatever your dad labeled you isn't true and doesn't define you. You know in your mind that you aren't a disappointment, damaged goods, or unwanted. But if you have heard a negative label repeatedly, chances are you subconsciously believe it to some degree. A label that was put on you can become lodged deep within you to the extent that it now defines you and affects every action you take. Who you think you are determines what you do.

The enemy loves for us to hang onto the past and fail to move on. One way he frequently attacks is by accusing us.[163] "You are unworthy. You are a disappointment. You are..." This is Satan's

---

[163] Revelation 12:10

"poker tell," as my pastor likes to say. If you are hearing accusations in the second person—"you, you, you"—this is likely the enemy's accusation. And he will find the thing that gets to you most and hurl it at you over and over again until he wears you down. This is why I can remember that hurtful thing a girl said about my outfit in the sixth grade. Or when my grandma made fun of my developing body and said I needed a better bra. Satan doesn't care what ammunition he uses to accuse you so long as it works. The enemy's goal is to confuse you about who God is and how He feels about you, just as he did to Adam and Eve. Remember, who you think you are determines how you act. So if you believe that you're damaged, dirty, unlovable or unworthy, that's how you'll live. That is Satan's goal. Jesus says that Satan is like a thief because he "comes to steal, kill and destroy."[164] Satan wants you to question your identity as God's beloved daughter so that he can derail your life. He wants you to believe that what you do or what has been done to you determines who you are. He even works through the world's culture, which encourages us to define ourselves. But that will never work. If we try hard enough, we can make ourselves look happy, successful, and beautiful on the outside; but we can't heal, cleanse, forgive, or free our souls. Only God can do that. And that's why He is the only one who can say who you are on the inside.

Without God, We Are Sinners

The word *sinner(s)* is used over forty times in the New Testament. The original Greek meaning refers to those who are "devoted to sin," and is "the most usual term used to describe the fallen condition of man."[165] In short, sinner describes someone before they become a Christian, before they receive forgiveness of sin and salvation from Jesus. *Sinner* is the default setting for all people who do not belong to God. In the Gospels, *sinner* was essentially a slur used by the

---

[164] John 10:10
[165] https://www.blueletterbible.org/search/Dictionary/viewTopic.cfm?topic=IT00 08207,NT0004598,VT0002646

self-righteous Pharisees against people they saw as unholy, idolatrous, nasty people. What galled them even more than the presence of such "sinners" was that Jesus befriended them.[166] Jesus said repeatedly that He came not for the righteous but for sinners. He said they were like sick people and He was the doctor who had come to heal them.

Ironically, the Bible turns things around and calls *the Pharisees* sinners: "Consider him who endured from sinners such hostility."[167] They repeatedly tried to trap Jesus, getting him into theological arguments that they thought they could win. When those attempts didn't work, they arrested him on false charges, sent him to a false trial, and murdered him. Jesus himself said, "See the hour is at hand, and the Son of Man is betrayed into the hands of sinners."[168] It was these hyper-religious people (who wrongly believed themselves to be the most holy people) who condemned Jesus to death. Though they looked holy on the outside, Jesus knew who they were sinners on the inside.

The Bible also tells us that sinners are people who only do good if they have something to gain from it.[169] Sinners need to repent or they will perish.[170] Jesus told three parables in which sinners were portrayed as things or people who were lost.[171] God does not listen to sinners.[172] Jesus is "holy, innocent, unstained, *separated from sinners,* and exalted above the heavens" (emphasis mine).[173] Sinners are also described as "double-minded," as their interests are divided between God and the world,[174] and they will receive God's judgment because they are against Him.[175] As you can see, the Bible categorizes sinners as people whose hearts are opposed to God. They are separated from God rather than in a relationship with him. This is who they are—

---

[166] See Matthew 9:9–13,11:19; Mark 2:15–15; Luke 5:30–33; 7:34–39, 15:1–10
[167] Hebrews 12:3
[168] Matthew 26:45
[169] Luke 6:32–34
[170] Luke 13:2
[171] Luke 15:1–10
[172] John 9:31
[173] Hebrews 7:26
[174] James 4:8
[175] Jude 1:15

this is their identity—and so the decisions and actions of their lives are opposed to God as well.

Label Exchange

Now for the good news. "God shows his love for us in that while we *were still sinners*, Christ died for us" (emphasis mine).[176] Did you catch that? "*We were sinners*." Past tense. When Jesus died for us, we were indeed in the sinner category I described at length in the above paragraphs. But we no longer are. Romans 5:19 says, "For as by the one man's disobedience the many were made sinners, so by the one man's obedience the many will be made righteous." While the sin of Adam brought sin into the entire human race, Jesus's life, death, burial, and resurrection on our behalf removes our sin and gives us his righteousness. Whereas a sinner is someone who's life is dominated by sin, someone who has been made righteous by Jesus is someone who obeys God and walks in his ways. He has made us righteous, and so we begin to live like that by the power of the Holy Spirit.

If you've spent any time in church, you've probably heard someone say, "I'm a sinner saved by grace." True, we are all born sinful and need God's love, grace, and salvation through Jesus. But did you know that once you become a Christian and receive the gift of salvation, the Bible no longer calls you a sinner but a saint? (We'll look at the term *saint* in greater depth in a moment). Those of us who belong to Jesus do in fact still commit sins (and we will until Jesus comes back and we are made like him), but we are not sinners.[177] That would be believing that what we do determines who we are. If you believe in the life, death, and resurrection of Jesus on your behalf, you are a forgiven child of God who sometimes sins and are growing in maturity by the power of the Holy Spirit.

Again, if it was your dad who gave you a derogatory or demeaning label, I am deeply sorry for that. It can be quite a challenge to

---

[176] Romans 5:8
[177] 1 John 3:2

believe that God doesn't view you in the same way. For example, one thing I hear women say quite often is that they are a "mess" or they are "broken." That they'll just give God what they can, messy parts and all, and that's okay. In one sense, this is true. God accepts us how we are. Jesus interacted with, healed, and saved many "messy" and "broken" people in the Bible. But He didn't leave them messy and broken. He forgave them, healed them, and sent them on to live a healthy, God-honoring life.[178]

I'll tell you right now, I don't feel like a mess, and I don't feel broken. I still sin and fail. I still deal with pain, struggles, and temptation. But I've been a mess before. Remember my "party girl" ways? I was not healthy emotionally, relationally, spiritually, mentally, or physically. I felt directionless, wounded, anxious, and alone. That, my friend, was a mess. That was how I acted when I didn't listen to who God said I was. Instead, I listened to the accusations of the enemy and called myself the things he whispered in my ear. And I can tell you from experience when you call yourself broken or messy, it's a self-fulfilling prophecy. You essentially limit yourself by believing a negative identity, and so you stay a broken mess.

When you belong to God through the work of Jesus, you are not a mess, and you don't have to stay broken. If you feel like a mess, maybe there are some areas in your life where you do need to make some changes. Maybe you need to consistently spend time with God and in the Bible. Maybe you need to get your health or your finances in order. Maybe there is someone you need to forgive or some pain you need to grieve with the Lord. If you truly do feel like a broken mess, pray and ask the Holy Spirit to specifically reveal to you what those areas are, and ask for His help to bring them into the order and peace that God provides. Not only does God want to heal the places of your soul that feel broken, He's the only one who truly can. "God is not a God of disorder but of peace."[179]

---

[178] For examples, see Jesus's healing a lame man in John 5:1–5 and the woman caught in adultery in John 8:1–11.

[179] 1 Corinthians 14:33

Another reason you may still feel like a broken mess (or insert any other negative label) is simply that you haven't taken off that label. The enemy does not want you to take it off. He will trick you, accuse you, and lie to you in order for you to continue to live your life with the label of "mess" stuck on you. He will attempt to obscure your God-given identity any way he can. Who told you that you are broken? Who told you that you are a mess? Who told you that you are _____? God didn't.

You are not destined for messy brokenness. When your Father looks at you, he doesn't see a mess. I have four little kids, so someone is always covered in food or dirt. Someone is always hurting themselves and running to me crying with tears and snot streaming down their face. I don't scowl at them and say, "Hmph. You are such a mess! You're hurt again? Oh well, I guess that's all you're capable of." I do not speak death and discouragement over them. Instead, I see sweet little kids, who are learning how to grow up, and that is a process that doesn't happen all at once. That is how the Father looks at you, and He speaks an identity of love, life, and forgiveness over you. You, my friend, are not a broken mess when you belong to Him.

What labels do you need to take off? Do you believe you are a failure, you'll never measure up, or you're not enough? Renounce that label by crying out to your Father. Pray that the Holy Spirit will help you to believe that Jesus paid the price for any and all sin you have committed in the past and will commit in the future and that your righteousness comes from Him alone. Do you believe you are broken, dirty, or damaged goods? Renounce that label as a lie. Pray and ask the Holy Spirit to help you believe that Jesus also died to cleanse you of the sin committed against you by others. Remember, only God gets to say who you are. And if you believe in Jesus, all of your negative labels have been destroyed once and for all.

With God We Are Saints

In studying all of the occurrences of "sinner" in the New Testament, I discovered something quite interesting. That word never occurs in either Acts or Revelation. Acts records the beginning and spreading of the early church after Jesus's ascension into heaven. Revelation records primarily the end-times when Jesus will return and bring God's plan of redemption to completion. Those books are full of Christians, but they are never referred to as sinners. There is another word used in those books, and indeed throughout the New Testament, for Christians. That word is *saint*.

The word *saint* is used sixty-one times in the New Testament to refer to Christians. The original Greek word *hagios* means that Christians are set apart for God and are exclusively his. "Just as God selected Israel as his people in the Old Testament and they called themselves saints, Christians in the New Testament are selected to belong to God and are called saints. That under the influence of the Holy Spirit they may be rendered, through holiness, partakers of salvation in the kingdom of God."[180] The original Greek word for saints also means pure, sinless, upright, and holy. In fact, the word *haggis* is also translated 161 times as "holy," and five times it is used to describe Jesus as the "Holy One."[181] What a contrast from the definition of sinner! In fact, a saint is the opposite of a sinner! The Bible contains more of these "opposites" that describe the dramatic change that happens when you become a Christian:

You were once God's enemy[182] but are now one of his chosen people.[183]

You were once lost but now you are found.[184]

You once had a heart of stone but now you have a heart of flesh.[185]

---

[180] BLB, Thayer's Greek Lexicon
[181] Mark 1:24, Luke 4:34, John 6:69, 1 John 2:20, Revelation 3:7
[182] Romans 5:10
[183] 1 Peter 2:9
[184] See the three parables Jesus tells in Luke 15.
[185] Ezekiel 36:26.

You were once marred by sin but now you are white as snow.[186]

You once belonged to the kingdom of darkness but now you belong to the kingdom of God.[187]

In fact, many times in the Bible, God literally gave people new names, thereby clearly giving them a new identity:

Abram (exalted father) became Abraham (father of a multitude).

Sarai (princess) became Sarah (noblewoman).

Jacob (supplanter) became Israel (God prevails).

Simon (hearer) became Peter (rock).

Saul (desired) became Paul (little).

When you become a Christian, the change is supernatural and miraculous. You don't just become a better version of yourself. You are not just a sinner who's been cleaned up. You are fundamentally, at your core, a new person! You are now a saint. "Therefore, if anyone is in Christ, he is a new creation. The old has passed away; behold, the new has come."[188]

Sinners' lives and hearts are dominated by sin, sinful desires, and self. When Jesus makes us new and removes the sinner label and instead brings us into the family of God, He gives us a new heart with new desires. Those new desires propel us to love God, read

---

[186] Isaiah 1:18
[187] Colossians 1:13
[188] 2 Corinthians 5:17

the Bible, serve others, apologize when we've wronged someone, be responsible with our time and money, extend forgiveness, and show compassion. When you belong to Christ, who you were is not who you are or who you will be when God is done with you.

When you belong to Jesus Christ, He removes your filthy garments—your negative labels—and clothes you in the finest of robes that reflect who you are to the depths of your soul.[189] You have been forgiven, cleansed, made completely new, and set apart by your Father to belong to Him forever. He loves you, delights in you, and is committed to you now and forever. And only He has the final word on who you are.

Heavenly Father,
Thank you that I belong to you
and that no one else gets to tell me who I am.
I pray that you would help me to renounce
any negative labels I still believe.
I don't want those lies to define my identity any longer.
Please help me to live in the truth that
I am your beloved, forgiven, cleansed daughter.
Thank you for sending your Son to make this possible
and for giving the Holy Spirit to help me walk forward in freedom.
In Jesus's name,
amen.

---

[189] See Zechariah 3:1–5.

15

My Heavenly Father Heals Me

My dad harmed me.

Being hurt and causing hurt are just part of being in human relationships. We are not perfect people and are bound to wrong another and cause pain from time to time. This is why forgiveness is a huge part of healthy relationships, as we'll discuss in a previous chapter. But what about harm? To harm someone means to inflict physical, mental, emotional, or spiritual pain upon them in such a way that the results are destructive. Harm is selfish and seeks to do damage to the other person. The effects of such harm often bleed into other areas of a person's life—other relationships, physical health, job performance, and mental outlook.

When a dad is the perpetrator of such harm, the effects can be deep and lingering. He damages and sometimes destroys his relationship with his daughter. Harm from a dad also distorts a daughter's view of God the Father. Whether she realizes it or not, a daughter who has been harmed by her dad often believes that God could potentially treat her the same way. This is clearly a lie but a lie that nonetheless affects every part of life. We're going to look at a dad in the Bible who sadly harmed his daughters in many ways and examine what impact that harm had in their lives. This man was Lot.

Lot was the nephew of the patriarch Abraham, and because Lot's father had died, he stayed with Abraham as they journeyed toward the land of Canaan. Abraham became very wealthy, and so did Lot. They eventually had to separate, as the land they were living on couldn't support their entire family and livestock. Abraham allowed Lot to choose which portion of land he wanted for raising his livestock. Lot chose the valley of Sodom and Gomorrah because its land was fertile and beautiful. At first Lot settled outside of town but eventually assimilated into the culture of the city, at least to some degree. Lot had taken a Sodomite wife, and they had children. His daughters were even engaged to be married to Sodomite men. We should note that 2 Peter 2:7–8 says that Lot was a righteous man who was tormented over the wickedness of the people of Sodom. Yet whatever he felt in his heart, he doesn't appear to have acted upon those convictions and ended up gravely harming his family.

Let's pick up the story in Genesis 19. Two angels (who appeared as men) were sent from God to rescue Lot and his family from Sodom before destroying the city for its evil ways. Lot had invited the men to stay at his house, and all the men of the city—both young and old—heard about the visitors. They mobbed Lot's house because they wanted to have sex with the men. Lot first tried to reason with the rabid crowd, but when that didn't work, he offered them his two virgin daughters. Perhaps Lot was bluffing and didn't think the men would take him up on his offer, or maybe he spoke without thinking because of the intensity of the moment. Either way, Lot offering his virgin daughters to a clamoring mob of sexually depraved men was completely inexcusable and cowardly. Instead of allowing Lot's daughters be victimized, the angels yanked Lot back into the house, barred the door, and struck the mob with blindness.

The angels then instructed Lot to gather the rest of his family and immediately flee the city because the Lord had sent them to destroy it. By morning, Lot still hadn't left, so the angels again urged Lot to flee, but the Bible says that "he lingered."[190] The angels extended God's mercy to Lot and physically grabbed him, his wife, and their two daughters by the hand and led them out of the city to safety. They were told to flee and not look back. Lot's wife did look back and died right there in the valley. Lot eventually ended up in a cave with his two daughters. Whereas he was once wealthy and set-

---

[190] Genesis 19:16

tled in the plains, he was now holed up in a cave with nothing. We can already begin to see the effects of Lot's bad decisions, and things got even worse.

Lot's daughters feared that there were no men left on the earth by which they could have children, so they made Lot drink wine until he apparently blacked out. The older one had sex with him the first night, and they repeated the whole ordeal so the younger one could have sex with him the next night. While it was the daughters' idea, Lot was no innocent victim. He was a grown man and became drunk of his own free will. He ought to have known that no good would from that. In fact, he should have been a father—a leader—and not put any of them into such an isolated or desperate situation to begin with. Going back even further than the situation in the cave, Lot seemingly didn't teach his daughters the ways of God but instead allowed them to be influenced by the sexually depraved culture of Sodom. The Bible says nothing more about Lot after this. His story ends here, but his family line does not. Both of his daughters became pregnant and gave birth to sons.

The story of Lot and his daughters is a tragic one. The Bible is full of people that we can learn from as an example, but sometimes what we learn is what not to do. From Lot, we learn five ways that dads can harm their daughters. And sadly, like Lot, sometimes dads cause harm in multiple ways.

First, Lot shows us how dads can harm their daughters *practically*. The passage in 2 Peter tells us that Lot hated how the Sodomites acted, yet he stayed there for over twenty years! It seems that Lot chose what was easy rather than doing what was right. This led to his own moral decline as well as harm to his family. Even when the time came to leave the city, Lot didn't obey right away. Instead the Bible says that he lingered. His daughters lost their fiancés in the destruction of Sodom. Their mother died as well. They lost all of their possessions, their livelihood, and ended up in a cave. Today, this could look like a dad who moves his family to another city, removing his kids from their schools, taking the family away from relatives, their community, and their church without taking into consideration where they are moving to. Where will they live? How will he make a living? Where will they worship? Who will be their friends and neighbors? What is the social and political climate like? This practical harm also results when a dad can't get his act together: he can't hold down a job, doesn't plan financially for the future, or pay attention to the reality of the family's circumstances and make healthy changes. The practical things of life matter greatly to our well-being.

Second, Lot harmed his daughters *relationally*. He married a woman from the idolatrous nation of Sodom and allowed his daughters to marry men from the city as well. These men were not godly men and died when the city was destroyed. Lot did not model or teach his daughters what a godly marriage relationship should look like. Furthermore, Lot betrayed his own relationship with his daughters when he offered them up to be to be violated by the crowd of rabid men. As I said before, Lot's actions here were totally inexcusable and cowardly. Lot treated the visiting angels, who were strangers, better than he treated his own daughters. Even if he was bluffing or spoke without thinking, his words still would have surely hurt his daughters. Just because they weren't harmed physically doesn't mean that they weren't harmed emotionally.

Have you ever felt like that? Sometimes we may see our dads act with professionalism and courtesy in business dealings or with friends and then act with harshness or apathy at home. Or worse, he may attempt to act "godly" while at church but very "ungodly" at home. We ask ourselves, "Why does my dad treat others better than he treats me?" When a dad damages his daughter relationally, this can impact her other relationships as well. It can be difficult to reach out to others when we struggle or to let them get close to us because we are afraid they might harm us as well.

Third, Lot shows us how dads can harm their daughters *spiritually*. Lot despised the actions of the Sodomites and was troubled at their wickedness. Yet he married a woman from the city, and he allowed his daughters to become engaged to men from that city. Lot's tolerance of such a wicked culture would surely have negated whatever Lot may have taught his daughters about God. Actions often speak louder than words. Furthermore, we know from Scripture that Abraham was close enough to see the city burning.[191] In fact, Abraham interceded on Lot's behalf and asked God to spare him when destroying Sodom. Lot likely could have returned to Abraham, but he didn't. It is very difficult to hold fast to your beliefs and convictions when you are isolated from God's presence and people and instead surrounded by an ungodly culture. As the spiritual leader of the home, a dad ought to settle his family in a place where they can meet with, worship, and live their lives in relationship with the family of God. Isolating the family from God's people causes spiritual harm.

Fourth, Lot hurt his daughters *generationally*. Lot raised his daughters in a godless city with wicked people and evil values. He committed the unthinkable and fathered his own grandsons. From these boys came two nations, the Moabites and the Ammonites, which were two of Israel's fiercest enemies. Lot's string of bad decisions and moments of cowardice changed the course of his family for generations to come. If Lot had heeded the angels' warnings and gotten his family out of the city, the future of his family could have been one of God's forgiveness and redemption. It could have been a future filled with joy and blessing instead of one filled with pain and strife.

Fifth, Lot shows how dads can harm their daughters *sexually*. If there is one thing that a dad should protect more fiercely than anything, it is his daughter's physical safety and sexual purity. Any sexual act between a dad and a daughter is entirely his fault and pure evil. As the first man in a daughter's life, a dad is to offer complete safety, appropriate affection, and not even a hint of sexual immorality. When a dad betrays this responsibility, he harms not only the relationship between his daughter and himself but he also harms her identity, her interactions with other men, and her view of God the Father. There is nothing more sick, more twisted, and more evil than a dad harming his daughter sexually. My heart breaks for you if your dad harmed you in this way. If you endured sexual abuse by your dad, I would encourage you to seek help from a godly counselor who can walk with you through the healing process. What happened to

---

[191] Genesis 19:28

you is real, but it does not define who you are nor is it the end of your story.

If you were harmed by your dad in any of these ways, I want you to know that your heavenly Father will not harm you.[192] When God created the world, there was no sin, death, or any harm in all of creation. Those things were brought to earth when the first humans, Adam and Eve, fell prey to the temptation of Satan. The enemy hates God and everything that God loves, so he spends all of his time waging war on the world and the people that God made. God has never changed, modified, or deviated from His plan for the world to be a place where we live in love, joy, harmony, and closeness with one another and with Him (we'll discuss God's plan for the world and for you in a later chapter). Through the power of Jesus's life, death, burial, and resurrection, God will redeem, renew, and remake all of creation in the end. There will be no more pain, sorrow, tears, or strife. *You* are part of that plan. Your Father loves *you* and wants to heal *you*. And you don't have to wait for Jesus's return to experience that healing. God can begin that work in you today, and He will bring it to perfect completion when you see Jesus face-to-face.

If you've spent any time in church, you have likely heard a lot about sin and repentance. It's true, we are sinners by nature and by choice. We do need to repent of our sin and trust in Jesus for our salvation, forgiveness, and cleansing. When we place our faith in Jesus's work on the cross on our behalf, we receive that salvation and are adopted into God's family in an instant. But what happens after that? What about the hurts we still carry? The fears we battle? The shame we still feel? There are wounds in our soul that don't get better with our repentance; they can only be healed by our Father and His love. I know this from firsthand experience.

For many years, I knew in my head that I was forgiven and loved by God, yet I still felt broken. This brokenness affected other areas of my life. I longed to have close relationships but didn't know how to connect deeply with people. I often felt anxiety when interacting with others. I would preplay and replay conversations with

---

[192] Jeremiah 29:11

159

people over and over in my head, either trying ahead of time to plan the perfect thing to say or reviewing the ways in which I felt like I misspoke. And in a single moment, while I was driving in the car (I usually hear from the Lord in the car or the shower. Probably because that's when I am still and my kids are quiet!), I realized that I felt as if I were walking through life with a limp. I felt wounded. So I prayed very simply, "Father, I want to feel healthy and whole." It was in that moment that I began to feel the Father's healing about my father wound. In that moment, I knew that He had been ready and waiting all along to draw close and heal me, and I was finally ready to let Him in.

Psalm 30:2 became very dear to me during that time of healing in my life. In it, David declares, "O LORD my God, I cried to you for help, and you healed me." The Merriam-Webster dictionary defines healing as making someone (or something) healthy, whole, or sound to restore them to health and render them free from ailment. Interestingly, the Hebrew word used in Psalm 30 for heal literally means "to sew together," and the sound of the root word imitates the sound of someone sewing quickly. I love this picture that God gives us in His word of what it looks like to receive His healing to our wounds. He wants to "sew up" our wounds, make us whole, and bring us into closer relationship with Him.

Beginning the journey of healing can be scary. Sometimes it's more comfortable for us to stay wounded. We get used to how we feel. We accommodate the hurt or compartmentalize it so it doesn't affect our everyday life. On the other hand, we can also nurse our hurt to the extent that becomes a twisted and intensified version of what actually happened. Some of us even befriend our hurt because it allows us to feel like a victim. You may have come to accept your hurt and believe that it will always be present in your life, but that's just not true. You do not have to settle for a wounded life because God is able and ready to heal you. My prayerful desire is that this moment would be a pivot in your life, a moment in which you begin to believe and receive your Father's healing love. I want to encourage you to take steps toward healing with three things I learned from my own journey.

Healing Is a Process

About twelve years ago, my car was struck head-on when another driver crashed into me. The other driver walked away from the scene while I was strapped to a backboard and taken to the hospital in the back of an ambulance. By God's grace, I only sustained soft tissue damage and didn't need any surgeries. I did, however, need almost a year of various therapies to regain the healthy body that I had before the crash. Twice a week I would go to an hour of physical therapy before heading to work. Other days, I would go to the chiropractor and massage therapist after work. I remember when it was one year to the day that the accident had occurred; I sat on the edge of my bed and sobbed. I was so tired of being sore from morning till night. I was exhausted from the hours, days, weeks, and months of treatment. I was tired of waking up every day knowing I was in my twenties but feeling as if I had the body of a ninety-year-old. I was weary, and it didn't seem like I was making much progress. I didn't know or feel it then, but my body *was* healing. God was using my treatments to sew my broken body back together one stitch at a time. Experiencing God's healing in our heart and soul often happens the same way, one stitch at a time.

The popular maxim "time heals all wounds" is actually a lie. There was no way my body would heal if I just gave it some time. Oftentimes if we wait to seek healing for a physical wound, it will fester or become infected. In the same way, healing in your heart and soul doesn't just happen if we give it time. Serious physical damage often takes quite a long time to heal under the skilled supervision of a medical professional. The same is true for healing our hearts. Healing only comes from time *with your Father*. Experiencing healing in my heart began by crying out to the Father and telling him I was ready to be healed. Then bit by bit, I gained His perspective on the father wound I was carrying. I began to trust that He loved me and would never forsake me. I believed that He would lead, guide, and provide for me. I also learned to forgive my dad step by step, stitch by stitch. Healing is a process, and the Father is the source of it all.

Healing Might Hurt

Healing my body after that car crash was a grueling process. Physical therapy pushed my body to the limit of what I felt it could do. Even the massage therapy was not the relaxing treat that I hoped it would be. It was truly painful! And yet, none of this pain was harming me. None of it was adding damage to my body. In fact, all of the pain that I experienced was part of the healing process.

God will never harm us. He will never act in such a way that causes damage to us and makes us unhealthy. He will, however, as a loving Father, allow us to endure some necessary pain along the road to healing. In my life, this meant revisiting some painful memories and talking about them with people I trust. It meant praying about fears, hurts, and anger that I had never given words to. Essentially, I went through a time of grieving. Although it was painful, bringing my grief before the Lord was the way through the pain and toward healing. Just like a doctor has to cut out a tumor to stop its effects on a patient's body, so, too, does the Father need to remove from us whatever is causing us harm. Only then is He is able to bring His healing truth and love to the deepest places of our heart and soul.

Healing Brings Joy and Praise

So what does healing look like? How do you know if you're healing? Using my car crash example again, I knew I was healing when I could begin to do the things I had done before the accident. I could take my dog on a walk! I could sit through a whole movie without experiencing back pain! I could pick up the little ones when I volunteered in kids ministry at church! Essentially, I felt more healthy than not healthy. Sure I had still had a bit of back-and-neck pain from time to time. But it was mild, and it didn't inhibit all of the healthy things I wanted to do. Healing in our hearts and souls is like that. There might be situations that bring up old memories, but instead of spiraling downward, we instead think, "Thank you, Lord, for how far you've brought me. Please help me to experience even deeper healing from this." There may be people who treat us poorly and we remember how our dad harmed us. But instead of dwelling on the hurt, we remember how passionately the Father loves us. We rejoice that we are His daughter, that He has healed us, and that He will continue to do so. One key indicator for me that I was healing up is that I could talk about my previous father wound with others. Your greatest pain often becomes your greatest ministry. That's why I'm writing this book. I know, to the depths of my heart, that the Father loves me, is for me, and that nothing can separate me from Him or His love. I'm not sure I would know this quite so well if I hadn't waded through pain to get here. Where my heart felt cut the deepest, the Father's love has filled it up to the point that it now runs over into love for others and praise for His name.

At the end of Psalm 30, David talks about healing like this: "You have turned for me my mourning into dancing; you have loosed my sackcloth and clothed me with gladness, that my glory may sing your praise and not be silent. O LORD my God, I will give thanks to you forever!"

My pastor says that when we experience pain, we also ought to look for the glory because even though the pain may seem heavy, there is nothing more weighty, powerful, and enduring than God's glory. So where is God's glory shining in your hurt? How has He replaced lies with His truth? How has He forgiven you? How has He cleansed you? How has He comforted you? What fears has He removed? How has He loved you?

If you feel the Holy Spirit stirring in you a desire to experience God's healing, that's a good thing even though it may feel a little scary. I would encourage you to first pray. Ask your Father to heal you. He wants to. He's ready to. I would also encourage you to find someone wise and trustworthy to walk with you through the process as a friend. This could be your husband, someone from your church, or even a professional counselor. Yes, healing may take time. Yes, it may hurt some. But your Father is the great Healer, and He wants to heal *you*.

Heavenly Father,
I feel broken and in need of healing.
I know you never will never cause me harm.
Please show me the specific areas in my heart and life
that I need to experience your healing.
I ask you to send your Spirit to guide me step by step
so that my heart will again be healthy and whole
and that I might sing your praise
and give thanks to you forever.
In Jesus's name,
Amen.

PART 3

Delicate Dads

16

My Heavenly Father
Is a Burden-Lifter

My dad was a burden-giver.

In Galatians 6:2 the apostle Paul says, "Bear one another's burdens, and so fulfill the law of Christ." However, just a few verses after this, he says, "For each will have to bear his own load." So which one is it? Do we carry our own load in life, or are other people supposed to help us? The key to this question lies in uncovering exactly what Paul means by the terms *load* and burden. Let me illustrate.

For my college orientation, we went on a three-day backpacking trip in the mountains in Washington state. I had a rather large backpack crammed full of everything I would personally need for the trek. Changes of clothes, food, sleeping bag, toiletries, and whatever else I needed (I honestly can't remember what else was in my bag because this was my first and last backpacking trip!) My backpack wasn't light, by any means, but it was bearable. My travel companions each had their own pack as well. None of us dared to pawn our bag off on someone else in the group. We each carried our own load.

This illustrates what the apostle Paul is talking about in Galatians 6:5 when he says, "For each will have to bear his own load." A load is something you can bear alone and that you have control over, something you alone are responsible for. Each of us has our own duties in life; things that we are personally required to do; and things that we possess the power to do on our own. For me as a wife and mother, my load includes taking care of our home, our children, spending time with God in His word, investing time in my marriage after the kids go to bed. I can't expect—nor would I want anyone else—to care for my husband and children in such an intimate way. These are the things that I am responsible for, and while they do take energy and discipline, they are doable.

Continuing with my backpack/load analogy, what would a burden look like? Several years ago, when my husband and I decided to move our family 1,400 miles from Seattle to Phoenix, we never once thought of cramming all of our belongings into a backpack. That would be absurd. We didn't even attempt to load all of our things into our minivan. Instead, we hired a moving company to transport our clothes, furniture, kitchen equipment, towels, toys, bicycles, and all the rest. This is a good image of what Paul means by a burden. A burden is an extremely heavy load beyond what you can bear alone. One of the great joys of being part of God's family is seeing Christians come to the aid of brothers and sisters who are dealing with life events that they cannot bear on their own. I have seen people bring meals, give money, pray for, and even just sit and listen to others who are suffering under the weight of heavy medical, financial, and relational difficulties. This is what Paul means when he says that we should bear one another's burdens.

Daddies Should Be Burden-Lifters

As parents, my husband and I want our children to grow and become increasingly responsible in their own lives. There are certain things at every age and level of maturity from childhood through adulthood that people ought to be responsible for. Our kids are learning to put away laundry, help with emptying the dishwasher, and keep their toys organized. These are things they can do on their own. But there are other things that they still need help with, things that feel like burdens to them. For example, my husband encouraged our daughters while they cleaned out the closet where we keep their art supplies. It looked like Hobby Lobby exploded in there. The girls were overwhelmed at the task and didn't know where to begin, so he coached them through each step of the process. He also boosted their enthusiasm by telling them, "Do you know how to eat an elephant? One bite at a time!" They got a good chuckle out of that and then proceeded with the task at hand. They felt positive, supported, and assisted by their daddy in doing a task that was too big for them to do alone. My husband (and I) wants our kids to grow in their capacity to take care of themselves, make decisions, deal with difficulties, and learn discipline. But he doesn't want them to feel crushed under the weight of the burdens in their life.

This is a silly but illustrative example of how a dad should be a burden-lifter. Dad should be someone you can ask for help when you're unsure of what do to in life or when things just feel like they are more than you can bear on your own. Dad should be a safe place for a daughter to seek guidance when she's in over her head. One of our daughters asked my husband, "How did you lift that trash can with just one arm?" To her, the trash can seemed immovable, but for her daddy it was easy. A daughter needs a dad who can lift the heavy trash cans in her life.

I also know of a dad who regularly takes his adult daughter out to breakfast and plainly asks, "What can I help you with? Is there anything or anyone I can pray for? Are there any burdens I can take from you?" And he always pays for breakfast too. God is a Father like this. He knows our weaknesses and wants to help us with the heavy things in life. Unfortunately, many of us grew up with a dad who either didn't help carry our burdens or made them worse. Let me share a few stories about women who had dads who were burden-givers rather than burden-lifters.

When Tanya was in college, she attended to school full-time, worked part-time, and had to take out student loans to pay for her tuition. During her junior year, she lived in a house with five other girls. That winter was extremely cold, and the electric bill ended up being astronomically high. Tanya was short about $50 to pay for her share. She called her dad and asked if he could lend her the $50, and the conversation went around and around. To her, $50 was a lot of money. To her dad, $50 wasn't much. He could have easily lent her what she needed, but she essentially had to beg for it. She felt so hurt that he cared more about $50 than about the fact that she needed help. This is just one example of a way in which the practical things we need to take care of in life can just become too much for us to handle alone. Tanya needed help and compassion, and she didn't get it. Not only did Tanya feel the weight of the extra financial burden, and she felt alone in dealing with it.

Jennifer also had a burden-giving dad. There were many times over the years that Jennifer and her dad disagreed or had differences of opinion in their relationship. Like in any relationship, for there to be reconciliation and hope of moving forward, both parties need to be willing to change. Both people need to apologize for their wrong-doing, ask for forgiveness, forgive the other person as well, and commit to change where necessary. Jennifer admits that she didn't do these things perfectly, but she did try. More often than not, she was met with a list of reasons why she was at fault and why her dad was not. Jennifer's dad was unwilling to take any responsibility for their struggles and was unwilling to change. For there to be any future in their relationship, Jennifer would have to adjust her behavior to meet her dad's demands. That is when Jennifer's responsibility for her part in the relationship shifted and became a burden. She felt as if her dad had backed up a truck and dumped the entire mess of their relationship onto her. There was no way that she could single-handedly clean up that mess.

Shannon's story is yet another example of a dad adding to his daughter's burdens. Shannon's dad had recently made some bad financial decisions and so had poor credit. As a result, Shannon's dad was not qualified to cosign on Shannon's brother's student loans, so he made her do it. If not for Shannon, her brother wouldn't have had money to go to college. In this situation, the dad took the place of a child, and the child had to take the place of the dad.

Sometimes dads fail to help us with practical burdens in our life. Sometimes they put emotional and relational burdens on us. Other dads burden their daughters by failing to carry their own load, leaving her to do what he is responsible for doing.

Projecting onto the Father

The effect that a burden-giving dad can have on our lives is that we come to believe that, at least to some extent, God is also a burden-giving Father. When facing difficulties in our lives—hurt from others, shame from our own sin, temptation, confusion, a big decision—we assume that if God didn't actively give the burden to us, at the very least He saw it and didn't care to help. We can wrongly believe that we are on our own, that God doesn't truly care about how we feel, and that life is just one hard thing after another. Have you ever felt like this? I have.

Several years ago, we moved into a new house within walking distance to our church where my husband also worked. We loved the neighborhood because we could walk to parks, shops, and restaurants. Our second daughter was a newborn, and we were just settling into being a family of four when my husband was offered a position at a different church location. It was a unique opportunity and required a unique skill set, which my husband possessed. Even though this opportunity was completely unexpected, my husband saw this as a stepping-stone into the future, as he would be given more responsibility and the ability to grow as a pastor. He trusted that this was the next step in a good plan that God had for our family, even though it didn't make sense to me. He felt at peace in his soul. I, however, thought this was just another time that I was getting dealt a bad hand. I literally said, "I guess because we're in ministry, I just have to suck it up and go along with this." I felt crushed under the weight of something I couldn't bear alone. My husband said that he understood that it was hard for me to uproot our lives after only being settled for a few months and having a new baby. He said it was completely okay for me to struggle but that if I started to lose hope, he'd get worried. It was only because of his hope and his certainty about the move that I didn't lose all hope. But at that point in my life, I didn't know God as a loving Father. I really did feel that God was mean and that I was alone.

That was one of the hardest seasons in my life to wade through, but I'm thankful for it now because it exposed a deep and ugly lie that

I had believed: God is a burden-giving Father and He doesn't care enough to help me. It was through delving into the Bible that the Holy Spirit shed light on this lie that I had believed and showed me that God the Father is ready, willing, and happy to lift our burdens.

Jesus Frees Us

Matthew 11:28–30 is likely a passage you've heard and read before. It's one of those "coffee cup verses" that shows up on mugs and bumper stickers, which in my opinion, robs it of its richness. Jesus says, "Come to me all who labor and are heavy laden, and I will give you rest. Take my yoke upon you, and learn from me, for I am gentle and lowly in heart, and you will find rest for your souls. For my yoke is easy, and my burden is light." Instead of leaving us alone to carry a burden that is much too heavy for us, God the Father sent Jesus to help us.

Jesus tells us to take his yoke upon us. A yoke is a wooden cross-bar that is fastened over the necks of two oxen and attached to the cart or plow they are to pull. Imagine you are one of these oxen. Now, if the other ox refuses to participate in carrying the load, you're stuck not only with the load yourself but also with partner who is making the whole situation worse. On the other hand, if you are attached to a strong, cooperative, and enthusiastic partner, your portion of the burden is bearable. Two oxen working together can carry more than each of them would be able to carry separately. Perhaps your dad was like the obstinate animal, and he made your burdens worse. The good news is that Jesus is the strong animal who walks with you every step and bears your burden with you.

In this particular passage in Matthew, Jesus is talking to people who were feeling the burden of religious legalism imposed on them by religious leaders. To this day, attempts to earn salvation through good works become nothing more than a burdensome yoke around our necks. When Jesus died on the cross and rose from the dead, He defeated Satan, sin, and death. That means He lifted the burden of sin you committed, of sin committed against you, of shame you carry, and the fears that plague you. God your Father does not want you to feel alone in bearing any burdens, especially the ultimate burden of sin and shame. So He sent Jesus to do it for you. Jesus lived the perfect life you and I cannot live, and He died the death that you and I deserve to die. He bore our ultimate burden on the cross, and now we are free.

This image of being yoked to Jesus as two oxen are yoked together to bear a load is a good picture not only of salvation but of how we ought to walk through life as well. I want you to envision whatever you feel burdened by. Maybe it's something in your life right now. Maybe it's something in your past or even in your future. Perhaps you feel an exterior burden stemming from a situation or relationship in your life. Perhaps you feel an interior burden, such as shame, rejection, or anxiety. Your burden is like the yoke. Imagine yourself as one of the oxen faltering under the weight of the yoke crossbar and see Jesus coming up beside you, lifting that yoke, and putting it on his back. Now see him taking your hand and the two of you getting up off the ground and moving forward together. You will still have to do the work and carry the load, but you will not do so alone. You will do it with the help, strength, and companionship of Jesus himself; and it will be fruitful in the end. Indeed, Jesus invites us to walk through life attached to him like this. He tells us to learn from Him and that He will be gentle with us. Because Jesus lived a fully human life and endured many hard things—even death on the cross—He can sympathize and help us when a burden seems to be more than we can bear alone.[193] No matter what the burden is, you can feel at rest in your soul because your Big Brother Jesus is carrying your burden with you.

Jesus Teaches Us

Jesus knows firsthand that being in a relationship with the Father will bring rest to your soul because He Himself lived his life that way. There are numerous times in the Gospels where Jesus went to a quiet place, away from the clamoring crowds, to pray and talk to the

---

[193] Hebrews 2:17–18, 4:15–15

Father. Jesus was fully human and felt burdens just like you and I do; He felt tired, angry, and sorrowful. There were people who wanted their own desires met by Jesus, and they tried to divert His attention away from what the Father had called Him to do. Just like you and I, Jesus needed to transfer those burdens to the Father in prayer and to receive power from the Holy Spirit to go forward. That's what prayer ought to be—us transferring our worries, fears, hurts, and sorrows to the Father so that we leave feeling unburdened and at peace in his love. Jesus was convinced that the Father loved him, was with him, and by the power of the Holy Spirit, would help him to get through what He could not envision getting through on his own.

Granted, "Pray, unload your bad feelings, then feel at peace and experience victory!" is not a formula. As Jesus did in his earthly life, we need to make a habit of praying to the Father to unload our burdens. First Thessalonians 5:17 simply says, "Pray without ceasing." Jesus's life was marked by frequent prayer to the Father, most notably in the garden of Gethsemane when Jesus prayed all night long before He was arrested, beaten, and crucified. And just like Jesus, when we pour out our hearts in prayer, we can transfer the burden that we feel to the Father and receive His love, peace, and presence in return. Then we will be able to endure what lay before us. God your Father is not a burden-giver who leaves you on your own. He's also not a passive dad who only makes himself available if you really need Him. He's an active, loving burden-lifter who sent Jesus both as an example and a companion to walk alongside your every step.

Jesus Leads Us

In Matthew 11, Jesus's invitation for anyone who feels burdened to come to him for relief and peace is given in a wider context that many often miss. So often in Christian teaching, we focus primarily on Jesus. And Jesus is vitally important, as the second member of the Trinity. But Jesus himself said that He is the way to the Father.[194] Jesus is not the destination; life with the Father is the destination.

---

[194] John 14:6

We see this if we go back to the beginning of the passage. Jesus actually begins by praying to the Father: "I thank you, Father, Lord of heaven and earth, that you have hidden these things from the wise and understanding and revealed them to little children."[195] Jesus is here saying that the people who are able to understand his message of salvation will have a childlike faith. That doesn't mean a simplistic or ignorant faith in which we are just expected to take God at His word and never have questions or struggles. Rather, a childlike faith is based on a relationship.

For example, my son is only two years old, yet he has tremendous faith in me. He doesn't worry about who will feed him or change his diaper or comfort him when he falls down. He knows I will every time and without fail. Why? Not because he is a child genius or because he knows so much about me. He doesn't even know my first name. But he knows I'm his mommy and he's my son. He knows that I love him, and that's enough. God the Father sent Jesus as our big brother to show us that our relationship with Him ought to be like the relationship I have with my son. Right before Jesus's invitation to come to Him when we feel burdened and weary, he says "No one knows the Son except the Father, and no one knows the Father except the Son and anyone to whom the Son chooses to reveal him."[196] Only then does He say, "Come to me..." Jesus the Son and God the Father have a warm, affectionate, intimate relationship, and the Father sent Jesus as our big brother to lead us into that kind of a relationship with Him as well.

Transfer Your Burdens

Let's go back to the image of Jesus carrying your yoke with you. Take a moment to consider the biggest burden that you are carrying right now. Imagine that you are handing it over to Jesus, emptying your hands of whatever is bringing you fear, distress, or pain. Jesus then stretches out his hand and grasps yours. You lift your eyes and

---

[195] Matthew 11:25
[196] Matthew 11:27

see Him looking at you with warmth, kindness, and love. "Come with me," He says, and the two of you begin walking along a dusty path that turns into a lush and beautiful garden. You continue walking for some time, with the sun warming your face, the birds singing, and the sweet smell of flowers drifting on a cool breeze. You come to a house, a mansion, really. In fact, it's the most amazing house you've ever seen. Jesus reaches to open the door, and there you see Him, your Father. His face breaks into a huge grin, and He opens His arms wide, surrounding you in the most loving, safe embrace you've ever felt in your life. The Father's loving arms eclipse any fear, stress, or burden you may feel. Those feelings are not gone; life must still go on, but you have peace and you do not feel alone. You know deep in your soul that you will forever be loved and safe with your Father.

Heavenly Father,
I confess that I have wrongly believed at times
that you are a burden-giver,
I pray that you would heal that part of my heart
and that I would believe in your love for me.
Thank you for sending Jesus to bear my burden of sin and shame.
Please send your Holy Spirit to renew my thoughts about you.
I want to come to you daily to unload my burdens
and to receive help and comfort in your embrace.
In Jesus's name,
amen.

17

My Heavenly Father
Is My Shepherd

My dad didn't protect me.

Dinah was a young teen when her family moved to a new town.[197] She had a large, complicated family. It all started when her father Jacob was a single young man and he went to live with his uncle Laban in order to find a wife. I'll spare you the intricate details of the story here,[198] but needless to say, he found more than a wife. Try two wives, two girlfriends, and thirteen kids. Jacob first married Dinah's mom, Leah. Then he also married Rachel (Leah's younger, prettier sister), Bilhah (Rachel's servant), Zilpah (Leah's servant). All of these women put together gave Jacob twelve sons, plus Dinah. I know, this whole situation sounds like a soap opera or some modern talk-show episode, but it's not. It actually happened and is recorded in the Bible! Dinah's father, Jacob, eventually decided that it was time to move his family back to his father's homeland in Canaan. On the way, they stopped in a town called Shechem. Jacob purchased a piece of land on which they pitched their tents, and he set up an altar to the Lord.

197

[198] See Genesis 29–31.

Shechem is a beautiful town situated between Mount Ebal and Mount Gerazim, thirty-four miles north of Jerusalem. The distance between the bases of these mountains is only five hundred yards. Shechem is tucked into this verdant, protected little valley and is the place where Jacob's great-grandpa Abraham had pitched his tent and built his first altar to the Lord.[199] This lovely town is also where the bones of Jacob's son Joseph were eventually buried. In addition, the well that Jacob dug at Shechem later became the well where Jesus met the Samaritan woman.[200] Both Jacob's well and the tomb of Joseph are still there to this day. There is, unfortunately, one huge dark spot in the significance of this little town in the history of God's people, and this is where we pick up the story of Dinah.

Dinah Ventures Out

Dinah's family settled just outside of Shechem on their way back to their homeland of Canaan. Genesis 34:1 says, "Dinah... went out to see the women of the land." Scripture doesn't tell us why Dinah ventured into town on her own, and so Bible commentators offer some possibilities. Some scholars say she wanted both to see and to be seen, that this was perhaps an act of rebellion. She knew she shouldn't be out on her own in a strange new town, but she didn't care. Other scholars attribute Dinah's going out alone to foolish wandering rather than rebellion. It may have been that she was just bored from being with her family all the time. She was the only girl in a house of twelve brothers after all. Maybe she just wanted to meet some other young women. In that day, it was not uncommon to see women out and about tending sheep or collecting water for the household. However, Dinah's leaving home alone seems to have had no other point but naive exploration. At this point in Dinah's story, it feels like watching a movie of a woman entering an abandoned building alone and thinking, "Oh, this is going to go badly." Dinah's

---

[199] Genesis 12:6–7
[200] See John 4

story did indeed take a dark turn. While she was in town, she caught the eye of powerful young man:

> When Shechem son of Hamor the Hivite, the ruler of that area, saw her, he took her and raped her. His heart was drawn to Dinah daughter of Jacob; he loved the young woman and spoke tenderly to her. And Shechem said to his father Hamor, "Get me this girl as my wife." When Jacob heard that his daughter Dinah had been defiled, his sons were in the fields with his livestock; so he did nothing about it until they came home. Then Shechem's father Hamor went out to talk with Jacob. Meanwhile, Jacob's sons had come in from the fields as soon as they heard what had happened. They were shocked and furious, because Shechem had done an outrageous thing in Israel by sleeping with Jacob's daughter—a thing that should not be done.[201]

Jacob's Nonreaction, the Brothers' Overreaction

Notice that Jacob says nothing in this passage. We gain no knowledge of his reaction to his daughter's rape. To be fair, some commentators say the custom at the time was that if a man had multiple wives, the responsibility of protecting a daughter fell to her full-blooded brothers.[202] This possibly helps to explain why Jacob "did nothing" about Dinah's rape until his sons came in from the fields. However, we do have other incidences recorded in Scripture of Jacob showing tremendous emotion, sorrow even, over his sons. In Genesis 37, Jacob's favorite son, Joseph, was sold into slavery by his brothers. The remaining sons faked Joseph's death and allowed Jacob to believe that a wild animal had devoured him. At this, Jacob mourned greatly.

---

[201] Genesis 34:2–7
[202] https://www.blueletterbible.org/Comm/jfb/Gen/Gen_034.cfm?a=34001

He tore his garments and put on sackcloth, signs of grief and mourning. His remaining children tried to comfort him, but he refused, saying that he would die from his grief.[203]

Again in Genesis 42, we have evidence of Jacob protecting his youngest son, Benjamin. This occurred after Joseph's brothers appeared before him in Egypt asking for food during the famine. They still didn't know the truth about Joseph's identity, yet Joseph commanded them to return home and bring their youngest brother to him. Benjamin was Joseph's full-blooded brother, for their mother had been Jacob's favorite wife, Rachel.[204] When the sons arrived home to collect Benjamin, Jacob told his sons, "My son [Benjamin] shall not go down with you [to Egypt] for his brother is dead, and he is the only one left." The only one left? He said this to his ten other sons! From this we see that Jacob is capable of strong, passionate fatherly feelings of love and protection but seemingly only for Joseph and Benjamin. The Bible does not record the same fatherly passion for Jacob's other sons or for Dinah.

We don't know if Jacob did anything to instruct Dinah about moving to a new town or if he tried to prevent her from going out alone. Maybe he did and she ignored him. No matter how she got there, the undeniable fact is Dinah found herself in great danger. Although Jacob was a great and godly man by the end of his life and became the father of the nation of Israel, this situation with Dinah seems to be one in which he could have done much more for his daughter. Even considering the custom at the time that the brothers were responsible for Dinah's safety, it is hard to believe that a dad would have no reaction to his daughter's rapist asking for her hand in marriage.

Jacob's sons took over the conversation, and they took things too far. Their righteous anger at the defilement of their sister turned into violent vengeance. They tricked Shechem into circumcising not only himself but also every single man in the town, saying that only

---

[203] See Genesis 37:34–35 (NIV).
[204] Genesis 35 tells of Rachel's death during childbirth with Benjamin.

then would they agree to the marriage.[205] Jacob still did nothing. While the men were recovering from their circumcision, Dinah's brothers Simeon and Levi stormed the city and murdered every man in the entire town, including Prince Shechem and his father Hamor. The rest of the brothers then joined them in plundering and looting the town. They took literally everything, including the women and children. Jacob still did nothing.

Jacob finally did say something, but only after great damage had been done to Dinah and destruction had been wrought on the entire town of Shechem. Instead of condemning the evil that was done to Dinah or that which his sons meted out on the town, Jacob laments that his sons' actions could bring trouble to him and his household. He fears that they will now themselves be a target for violence at the hands of the surrounding nations. He denounces not the wrongs done but the only consequences that could follow. Jacob only gets angry when he realizes that he and his household might suffer because of what his sons did.

We don't know how Dinah felt throughout this tragic series of events. In fact, not one word of hers is recorded. Yet I think we can imagine how she might have felt. A daughter who likely just wanted to experience something new got in over her head and found herself in a dangerous situation that she wasn't able to get out of. Perhaps Jacob could have stopped her. Perhaps not. But even after it all happened, he didn't defend her or seek justice for her. He didn't tend to her or rescue her. Dinah's brothers were the ones who brought her back home. Jacob's only recorded words about the entire ordeal were his fears of what might happen to him and his household as a result. I can't imagine that Dinah felt very loved. Jacob seemed to be a man who loved God and wanted to please Him. He was a man who received God's grace over and over again. However, that doesn't mean that he was a perfect man or a perfect dad. The good news is that God was a perfect Father both for Dinah and for Jacob. If you

---

[205] Circumcision was a symbol of purity and the sign that God's people belonged to Him. Dinah's brothers said that to give Dinah in marriage to someone uncircumcised would be a disgrace. They used a holy sign given by God for unholy purposes.

can relate at all to Dinah's story, I want you to see that whatever hurt your dad may have caused you by failing to protect you, God is a perfect Father who will never let you down.

God Is My Shepherd

One of the pictures the Bible uses to illustrate what our relationship with God should be like is that of a shepherd and his sheep. Throughout both the Old and New Testaments, the Bible uses this shepherd imagery because sheep were important in ancient times. Back then sheep were used for food, clothing, sacrifices, and payment of taxes. Sheep are not as integral a part of most societies nowadays, but we can still learn from this analogy. Sheep are completely docile, dependent creatures. No one is afraid of a sheep. Today, we have children's songs about sheep, we count sheep to fall asleep, and we put them in petting zoos. Sheep are not known for their toughness or their wits. Left to themselves, sheep would quickly become lunch for a hungry predator. Because sheep are so defenseless, the job of a shepherd is crucial to their survival. If not for the shepherd's protection, the sheep would not survive. Sheep are thus used in Scripture as a symbol of God's people; we are supposed to be meek, humble, and follow His leading. The best image of this shepherd and sheep relationship is seen through the person and teaching of Jesus because one of the things Jesus was sent to earth to do was to show us what the Father is like and how to have a relationship with Him.

Your shepherd names you. Jesus said, "The sheep hear his [the shepherd's] voice, and he calls his own sheep by name and leads them out...the sheep follow him, for they know his voice. A stranger they will not follow, but they will flee from him, for they do not know the voice of strangers."[206] Many shepherds do indeed give each of their sheep a unique name, and just like a dog, they come when called. It is true that sheep will not follow the voice of someone they don't know. Not all the sheep in a flock are all domesticated. Sometimes there are sheep in a flock that are still wild, but they can be taught their names

---

[206] John 10:3,4, 5

and learn to follow their shepherd.[207] God's Spirit speaks to you just as personally and uniquely as a shepherd calling his sheep by name. You, too, can learn to respond to His call. Do you hear the voice of your Shepherd? Do you respond to His voice?

Your shepherd leads you. A shepherd usually walks ahead of his sheep, and because they know and trust his voice, they follow. Jesus said, "When he [the shepherd] has brought out all his own, he goes before them, and the sheep follow him.[208]" Sometimes, if necessary, the shepherd will drive his sheep from behind in order to get them where they need to be. God can nudge us onward like this too. Sheep are not great at keeping tabs on their surrounding environment. They are simple-minded. They don't know *where* to go. They don't know *how* to get there. Left to themselves, they'd be sitting ducks for predators. We are not unlike sheep in that we cannot possibly know as much as our Father, nor can we be in control of things like He alone is. We need His leading every day of our lives.

Your Shepherd Nourishes You. Psalm 23:1–3a (NLT) says,

> The LORD is my shepherd, I have all that I need. He lets me rest in green meadows, he leads me beside peaceful streams. He renews my strength." Sheep need their shepherd to locate places with grass to eat and water to drink. They need their shepherd to know when to pause their journey and let them rest. This is what God our Shepherd does for us. He gives us his Word to nourish our soul. He gives us strength when we need it, comfort when we need it, peace when we need it. Jesus, who called himself the "good shepherd" said that he came that we would not only have life, but have it abundantly.[209]

---

[207] Smith's Bible Dictionary. https://www.biblestudytools.com/dictionaries/smiths-bible-dictionary/sheep.html

[208] John 10:4

[209] Se John 10:10

God your Shepherd wants you to flourish, and He provides everything you need for that to happen.

Your shepherd defends you. After a day of grazing in the pasture, a shepherd brings his sheep back into the fold at night. This fold is a fenced enclosure sometimes built against the wall of a home or another building. The shepherd inspects and counts each sheep as it comes through the door. He then closes the door and guards it all night long. If a robber or predator wants to get to the sheep, they would have to get past the shepherd first. Jesus tells us that He Himself is the door through which anyone has to pass if they wish to get to us.[210] Through His Word and His Spirit, God protects us from wolves: false teachers who espouse doctrines contrary to God's truth, as well as religious people who would have us believe that God cares more about our following rules than He does about our relationship. God also protects us from ourselves, including areas of weakness, pride, and temptation. When you belong to the Father through Jesus Christ, nothing can separate you from Him. Your relationship with God is secure because of what He has done to save you and what He continues to do to keep you safe in his fold. Nothing in the universe can separate you from the loving embrace of your Shepherd.[211]

Your Shepherd pursues you. My husband and I were at an outdoor water slide park a couple of years ago. We had our three young daughters with us, and I was nearly nine months pregnant with our son. We were all playing at a kid's splash pad area when we suddenly realized our three-year-old was gone. I stayed with the other two girls, begging the lifeguards to look for our missing daughter. My husband tore through that park, looking everywhere, telling the lifeguards to bar the doors and to call her name over the loudspeaker. We have never been so terrified in all of our lives. The lifeguards were calm, saying, "There's no way she can get out. We'll find her." They were so calm because it wasn't their child who was missing! We, on the other hand, were desperate to find her! It seemed like an eternity, but it was probably only a couple of minutes before my husband found

---

[210] See John 10:9
[211] See Romans 8:39

her. She just wanted to try the water slides, wandered that direction, and then realized she was lost. She was a sobbing mess by the time her daddy got to her. All of us were beyond relieved and grateful that she was safe back in our arms. God goes after wandering sheep like that, sometimes even saving us from ourselves.

Jesus told a parable in Luke 15 in which a shepherd left his ninety-nine safe sheep to go find the one that was lost. When the shepherd finally found the lost sheep, it was feeble and weak. So the shepherd carried that sheep home, rejoicing that the one who was lost was now found. This, Jesus said, is what it's like when a sinner repents and becomes a part of the family of God. Though Jacob showed no emotional reaction upon learning of Dinah's rape, this parable teaches us that one little lost lamb who has been brought back home to God is cause for full-scale celebration. God is a Father who acts to protect you and reacts with joy when you are safe in his embrace. How far has your Shepherd gone to find you and bring you home?

Your Shepherd sacrificed for you. In Jesus's time, being a shepherd was a tough job, and it was not usually seen as a noble profession in society. It involved hardship, a nomadic lifestyle, having to forage for food, and only possessing what could be carried on one's back. Being a shepherd also meant facing certain danger, whether from wild animals or menacing robbers. David is a prime example of this. Long before he became king, even before he slew the giant Goliath, he risked his life to rescue sheep that were taken by predators. In order to save his sheep, David had killed lions and bears.[212] That is a shepherd's heart. No matter the risk to himself, David was not willing to let even one of his sheep die.

This is why God your Father sent Jesus your Big Brother to be your substitutionary lamb and rescue you out of the jaws of Satan, sin, and death: "He was oppressed, and he was afflicted, yet he opened not his mouth; like a lamb that is led to the slaughter, and like a sheep that before its shearers is silent, so he opened not his

---

[212] See 1 Samuel 17:34–36

mouth."[213] Your Father did not spare even his own Son but sacrificed him in your place so that you can stay safe in His fold. Jesus is not only our Good Shepherd, but He was also the ultimate sheep, not only for His sacrifice but for His unwavering obedience to the will of the Father and trust in His love.

The Father's Shepherd Heart

One of my favorite scriptures showing God as our shepherd is Isaiah 40:11: "He will tend his flock like a shepherd; he will gather the lambs in his arms; he will carry them in his bosom, and gently lead those that are with young." In this verse, God gives us an image of a strong yet tender shepherd who cares for, leads, and protects his sheep so they will flourish. This is not a picture of a harsh taskmaster or owner who sees his sheep merely as property. Nor is this a picture of a hired hand, who does not own the sheep and so flees when there is trouble.[214] Unfortunately, Jacob acted more like a hired hand than a shepherd. The Bible records no reaction from Jacob after learning of Dinah's rape; Jacob doesn't intervene when his sons plunder an entire town; his only concern is retaliation they might face from surrounding nations. This is ironic because he was in fact a shepherd by profession. However, it seems in this stage of his life, Jacob didn't have a shepherd's heart.

The picture that Jesus paints of a shepherd and his sheep is one of relationship. A shepherd's entire daily life is carried out in such a way as to care for, protect, and guide his sheep. Sheep would not survive without their shepherd; they trust and follow him. In the same way, God doesn't give you a set of rules to follow in order to be acceptable to Him nor does He merely use you to accomplish things for His kingdom. He really doesn't need your help. God loves you, knows you, and speaks to you through His Word and His Spirit because He wants you to have an abundant life. He also knows that

---

[213] Isaiah 53:7
[214] John 10:12–13

you cannot have an abundant life apart from Him. Like sheep, your role is to trust and follow your Shepherd.

If, like Dinah, you feel your dad didn't protect you like a shepherd, you may struggle to learn to follow God and trust his protection. Let me encourage you with two things. First, just because your dad may have failed to protect you doesn't necessarily mean he doesn't love you. We know that Dinah's father, Jacob, was a man who met with God, who worshipped God, and who often received God's grace. People can be Christians and love you and still fail you. What is best for both you and your dad is to forgive him and to pray for him. Chances are, if he wasn't a good shepherd to you, he might now know God as his Shepherd. Second, even though your faith in your Father may feel small and feeble, that's all right. If your faith is genuine, He can work with that. Just like sheep can learn the voice of their shepherd, you also can learn to recognize and follow the voice of your Shepherd. God is the safest being in the universe, and even if you falter or stray, He will not lose you.[215] When you are a sheep under His protection, nothing can take you from Him. You will be, now and forever, safe in His fold.

Heavenly Father,
I have not felt safe or protected for a long time.
Thank you that you are my Shepherd
and that even when I haven't realized it,
you have been protecting, leading, guiding, and feeding me.
Please help me to hear, trust, and follow your voice.
In Jesus's name,
Amen.

---

[215] See John 17:12.

18

My Heavenly Father Is the Best Leader

My dad wasn't a leader.

The classic dad character on a family sitcom is usually some version of the same cliché. When he's not at work, he spends most of his time sitting in his "dad chair." Sitcom dad almost always has a bit of a paunch belly on a body shaped like turnip. He's often outsmarted by his wife and kids. Mom doesn't respect dad, so neither do the kids. He's there to bring home the bacon, put food on the table, and serve as an occasional source or subject of a joke. In fact, he is a joke. Sitcom dad is a stereotype to be sure. But you know what they say. Stereotypes exist because to some extent, they are true. If nothing else, the existence of the sitcom dad character reveals what many people think about dads: they aren't really necessary because they don't do very much.

The bottom line is that instead of being the leader of the family, sitcom dad just kind of exists and lets mom and the kids figure out everything for themselves. Some of us grew up with a non-leader dad like this. Sometimes this type of dad would rather be his kids' friend than their father. He doesn't do the hard but crucial work of instructing, correcting, and guiding his kids. He'd rather let the bad behavior slide and avoid potential conflict than wade through a difficult situation, so he leaves the discipline to mom.

The nonleader dad sometimes enables his kids. For example, I know a dad who allows his teenage son to continue living with the family, even providing him with a car, despite the fact that the kid is dealing drugs at the local high school. This dad is not a leader but an enabler of bad behavior. The nonleader dad neglects to teach his daughter about men or dating and then is shocked when she picks a bad guy. In fact, many young women who have weak dads seek out men who are strong, even if that means they are "bad boys."

Sometimes a nonleader dad isn't in control of the family's finances, his own emotions, or his flesh (abuses alcohol, food, etc.). This type of dad often struggles to get out ahead of things—the car is always needing repairs, the bills are unpaid, the kids are wearing clothes that are worn out or too small. His life is a reaction to circumstances, and he can't figure out how to get on top of things.

The problem with having a dad who isn't a strong, godly leader is that he creates a leadership vacuum. Sometimes mom steps in and tries to lead the family. Moms and their influence in a child's life are invaluable, but mom isn't dad no matter how hard she tries. Nor does mom replace dad, even though our current culture says moms and dads are interchangeable.

Another possible result of dad not leading the family is that the kids attempt to figure life out for themselves. In the absence of a godly dad who leads them, kids look elsewhere for someone to lead them; they look for someone who can provide them with direction on what to believe, what to value, what is true, and what to pursue in life. While some kids do find other godly men to look up to who bring them to church and teach them about God, most kids don't. Today, most teachers and school counselors are women. I know many wonderful women educators, and I am so thankful for them, but they simply can't fill the void left by a child's dad. When dad doesn't lead the family and seek to follow God's ways, the whole family suffers.

I want to take a moment and acknowledge that if any of this describes your dad, it is likely that he didn't have a good example of fatherly leadership in his life. I don't say this to let him off the hook but to encourage you toward understanding. Your dad may have done the best he knew how, even though his "best" negatively affected you. God is the Father who both you and your dad need.

The Family "Kingdom"

God created everything—the sun, moon, planets, galaxies, and everything in them. He set the laws of nature in place. He has determined the rhythms of life, and He keeps it all going. As the only Being who has no beginning and no end, and as the sole Creator, He is the Leader over all places, times, and peoples. When God finished his creation work, He declared everything that he had made to be "very good." God's intention for the people He made was to follow His ways, create families; steward and enjoy the Earth; and dwell with Him forever. That was the plan before sin entered the world, and that is still God's plan. Through the person and work of Jesus, God will once again bring us to a place where everything is "very good" and all of His kids live with Him and follow His ways. (We'll go much more in-depth on this in a following chapter.)

My husband and I tell our kids, "God made the world. He made you and loves you, so He knows how life works best." This is what makes God the best Leader there ever has been or ever will be, and this is why all other leaders ought to lead like Him. There is no one like Him. The way that things are in God's kingdom are the way that things are supposed to be. We are supposed to be living in a relationship with God that is unbroken by sin in a world that is unmarred by the curse. God's kingdom is supposed to be normal; the world and its culture are not normal. That is why Jesus said to pray, "Our Father in heaven, hallowed be your name, your kingdom come, your will be done, on earth as it is in heaven."[216] Sin has corrupted our world and ourselves, but God's kingdom, His ways and His leadership over all things has no beginning and no end. God's kingdom is a place where He alone rules with perfect, loving leadership; where people don't sin against God or against one another; a place where there is no pain, tears, temptation, or fears. God's kingdom is a place a perfect love,

---

[216] Matthew 6:9–10

harmony, peace, safety, closeness, enjoyment, and adventure. This is the environment in which He lives today in heaven and the way things will one day be again for us when Jesus returns. For now, we get to see, experience, and participate in glimpses of God's perfect kingdom as we love and follow Him.

God's design is that husbands and fathers would reflect His leadership and His kingdom as they lead their "family kingdom." Yes, moms are leaders in the home too. But as the God-appointed head of the family, the dad is the primary leader. Dads create the family kingdom—that is, the environment—that kids grow up in, interact with, and learn to accept as normal. The family kingdom is where kids learn what to believe in, what to value, how to act, and how to interact with others. When dads seek to follow God and his ways, the family kingdom does reflect something of God's kingdom, and kids learn that this is how life was designed to be. They learn that God is the best Leader with the best kingdom. When dads don't model the family kingdom after God's kingdom, the family veers from God's design. The result is that kids don't know that God is in charge, and that this is a good thing! Let's break this down and look at three ways that a dad's leadership creates the family kingdom for better or worse.

First, dads lead the family kingdom *practically*. As leaders of the family, God has appointed dads to be responsible for choosing where the family lives, where they will attend church, who their friends will be. These practical decisions are much more significant than they might seem. Your life will be very different if you live in a safe neighborhood, near a good Bible-teaching church, and in a place that is affordable in comparison to a place that is hostile to Christianity, incredibly expensive, and not near a godly church community to be a part of. We found this to be the case when we moved our family from Seattle to Arizona. Seattle is becoming increasingly liberal and expensive, which means it is quite difficult for a family of six to live on a single income. Arizona is much more affordable, has many good choices for schools, and is much more accepting of Christianity. When we were first married, my husband and I loved living in Seattle. We loved to attend concerts, eat at amazing restaurants, and explore the city. After we had kids, our priorities changed.

My husband decided we needed to move to a place more suited to children and families, and I fully agreed. We have lived in Arizona for several years now, and moving here was one of the best decisions we have made for our family.

Second, dads lead the family kingdom *culturally*. What I mean by "culture" in this sense is twofold: what dads teach and what dads tolerate. In our home, we teach our kids to value what God values. We teach our kids to love God and love others. We teach our kids that they are to be servants rather than selfish. We teach our kids that God's way is the best way, so we read His Word to discover more about Him and how He designed the world to be. We teach our kids that it's important to make memories and have fun because God is fun!

We also have some things in our house that we do not tolerate. We do not let our children "keep score." For example, it's okay that one child went with Mommy to the grocery store today; someone else will have a turn tomorrow. I know your sister took the toy you were playing with, but she gave it back and apologized. We don't keep a record of wrongs. We don't tolerate grudges. We don't use our hands against one another. We solve a problem, forgive, show grace, and move on. We don't tolerate fussing. If a child chooses to fuss, they do so alone in another room. By teaching our kids *what we do want* and *not tolerating what we don't want*, we are creating a home kingdom in which we love and serve both God and one another. It is a process that gets messy, loud, and complicated sometimes; but we are making progress.

Finally, dads lead the family kingdom *relationally*. Whether dads realize it or not, they set the temperature of the home. Some homes are cold and relationally distant because that's how dad is. Other homes are hot, tense, and angry because dad is like that. Ideally, the temperature of the family kingdom will be warm. The family should be a place where relationships are loving, fun, affectionate, and close. Let me give you an example of what this looks like. In our house, my husband has taught our kids three rules that we learned from our pastor: be safe, have fun, and love each other. Part of my wants to add a fourth rule—pick up your stuff! (And all the moms said, "Amen!")

Most of our kids' conflicts or struggles to obey fall under one of these three rules. But here's the crucial thing to see about these rules: they are made to enhance and grow our family relationships. They are not rules for the sake of rules nor are they rules made at the expense of relationships. They are rules that create an environment in which our relationships can grow and thrive.

This might be a new way for you to think about leadership. Most often we think of leadership in the sense of making decisions and moving forward with a plan. But if we stop and think for a moment, most of us know instinctively that leaders of other organizations or groups create the kingdom in which the group operates. For example, CEOs, coaches, and teachers communicate the beliefs, values, goals, and codes of conduct for their respective groups. But by and large today, most people in our world don't see the God-given role, and indeed incredible value, of having a dad that sets a godly environment for the family. The phenomenon of dads voluntarily abdicating their leadership role in the family has become an exponentially increasing problem in recent decades (what with at-will divorce, children born out of wedlock, and culture's attempt to redefine marriage and family). Nevertheless, the problem of dads who do not act as the leaders of their family is as old as humanity.

Truth be told, many well-known men in the Bible were not great dads. The first dad in the history of the world, Adam, stood idly by while his wife Eve succumbed to the serpent's temptation and ate the forbidden fruit; the result was the fall and cursing of all of Creation. Their children, Cain and Abel, were the first children on the planet. From the first sibling rivalry in the history of the world also came the first murder: Cain killed Abel out of jealousy. It seems as if Adam didn't lead his wife or his children very well, even though he began his life in the Garden of Eden in the presence of God.

Another example of a dad who's weak in leadership is Jacob, whom we will discuss in greater detail in a subsequent chapter. Two of his sons killed all the men in an entire town as revenge for the rape of their sister Dinah. As a young man, Jacob himself was a trickster (Jacob conned his older brother Esau out of his birthright) who was later tricked by his own sons. Jacob showed such favoritism to

Joseph, that his other *eleven* sons sold Joseph into slavery in Egypt and faked Joseph's death, causing Jacob great grief.

The great and mighty King David, who killed a lion and bear with his own hands, slew the giant Goliath, and killed tens of thousands of men in battle seemed to have little influence over his own children. David had sons who killed other sons, tried to claim the throne for themselves, and one son who raped his half sister among other heinous offenses. David is unfortunately an example of how men can achieve great success in their professional life yet greatly fail in their personal life. The Bible is full of people just like us—deeply flawed yet loved, forgiven, and empowered by God for no good reason other than His love for us.

If you had a dad who wasn't much of a leader, you might struggle to understand God as the Leader of your life. There are so many things we could discuss regarding God's leadership over humanity, creation, and so on. But I don't want to have a merely theological discussion. Instead I want to give you some helpful instruction so that you don't see God merely as a distant creator who issues commands from afar but rather as your tender yet powerful Father who displays his loving leadership over your life every day.

Six Helpful Truths About God's Leadership

First, the Father's leadership is relational. During the last supper with the disciples, Jesus had many things to say to prepare them for what they were about to witness—his death, burial, resurrection, and ascension back to the Father in heaven. One of the things He says is that they need not worry about His leaving because He is going to prepare a place for them in his Father's house. Not the Father's team, organization, nation, or commune. No, God has a house because He is a Father with children. Jesus our Big Brother is preparing space just for you. Jesus also says, "And if I go and prepare a place for you, I will come again and take you to myself, that where I am you may be also… I am the way, and the truth, and the life. No one comes to the Father except through me."[217] As the Leader over all the universe, the Father's desire is that at the end of this messy world, at the end of your life, you would live with Him in His house. God the Father is orchestrating all of human history so that every one of His kids will have an eternal home with him.

Second, the Father's leadership is personal. So many of us know Psalm 139:13–14 which says, "For you formed my inward parts; you knitted me together in my mother's womb. I praise you, for I am fearfully and wonderfully made." We probably also know Luke 12:7, "Why, even the hairs of your head are all numbered." I fear that these verses can become so familiar that they lose their beauty and power. So let me tell you a story about a friend of mine. She had been close to her dad all of her life until just a few years ago. Every year at Christmas, her dad would give her a box of a specific brand of chocolates. However, a few years ago an issue arose in their relationship. Although my friend was willing to work things out, her dad was not. Sadly, they haven't spoken for some time, and she hasn't gotten her Christmas chocolates for a few years. Unknown to my friend, another friend had prayed that God would send her a sign that He is her Father and that He loves her deeply. I kid you not, the exact brand and flavor of chocolates that my friend would receive from her dad showed up in the mailbox. No one ordered them for her, no one knows where they came from. I like to think that somehow the Father sent her a personal message of "I love you." See? God's sovereignty isn't an impersonal thing. He isn't a distant king. He's a Father who is sovereign even over chocolates and the mail system and can use them to send a message of love to a daughter who needed it.

Third, the Father's leadership is for your good. I struggled for many years thinking that God's leadership in my life meant that when hard things came, I had to just grin and bear it. I thought being a Christian meant simply living for God's glory. Indeed, it does. But what I didn't realize is that God's glory and my good are not separate; they are one in the same. Recall from a previous chapter when I talked about our family's move to a town I didn't like at all. I felt as if

---

[217] John 14:3,6

God just expected me to "do my duty" as a pastor's wife. My husband didn't like the town very much either. But instead, he believed God was a good Father and that this move was our next step. We both hoped this town wasn't the end zone, truth be told. And it wasn't. My husband was right. The move was just a step in a series of events that got us to where we are now. Looking back, I can see God leading us step by step to the life we now have, which is far beyond anything I could have dreamt.

In Deuteronomy 6, Moses gave the Israelites something of a farewell address before he died. He reminds them that the reason they are to obey God's commands and teach them to their children and grandchildren so that "your days may be long…that it may go well with you, and that you may multiply greatly…in a land flowing with milk and honey."[218] God's leadership in our lives is for our good and for our enjoyment of Him.

Fourth, the Father's leadership is unstoppable. In the book of Genesis, Joseph's brothers hated him because he was their father Jacob's favorite son. The brothers faked Joseph's death and sold him into slavery in Egypt. While he was there, Joseph was accused of a crime he didn't commit and thrown in jail. Eventually, through a series of miraculous events, Joseph was given a prominent position in Egypt as the head of Potiphar's household. Potiphar was the captain of the palace guard, so Joseph's position was powerful indeed. Nothing could explain Joseph's going from a prisoner to a powerful leader apart from the hand of God.

Years later, when Joseph's brothers came to buy grain in Egypt because there was a famine in their land, they unknowingly appeared before Joseph. When he made his identity known to them, they were afraid, for they knew they had sinned against him greatly. Joseph's response was amazing: "As for you, you meant evil against me, but God meant it for good, to bring it about that many people should be kept alive… So do not fear, I will provide for you and your little ones."[219] When people sin against us, when we suffer the effects of

---

[218] See Deuteronomy 6:1–3
[219] Genesis 50:20

a fallen world, it is not God's doing because there is no darkness or evil in Him. Yet He is so powerful and so loving that he can even use evil for our good. Even if we are the ones who fail and fall, He is faithful. God cannot lose any of his kids, and that includes you.[220] Nothing can separate you from God's love.[221] Nothing can stop His good plans for you.

Fifth, the Father's leadership is paradoxical. God's leadership is both big and small. It is both in miraculous physical healing and a whisper from the Holy Spirit. It is both cosmic and specific. God is the one who holds each atom of the universe in perfect order, and He is the one who provides a friend when you need one. We see God's leadership in both mysterious and obvious ways. Only He sees a baby growing in the womb while we all can see His glory when someone becomes a Christian and completely turns their life around. Let's not miss seeing and praising the loving Father's leadership over the world and over our lives because He doesn't always show it in the way we expect it.

Finally, the leadership of the Father is current. The Bible tells us how God spoke the world into existence. That He made Adam from dust. That He parted the Red Sea and led the Israelites through in on dry ground. We know that He fed His people with manna from heaven for forty years in the desert wilderness and that countless Old Testament prophecies about Jesus were fulfilled completely. Yet I fear that we can become jaded by these "Bible stories." We sometimes don't realize that these things, and countless other events in Scripture, actually happened. Too often we don't realize that God is still displaying His loving, powerful leadership over creation and humanity.

We know a man who was recently was in a small plane crash. By all accounts, he should be dead. There is no explanation for why his femur broke in multiple places, yet his femoral artery was untouched. If it had been punctured, this man would have bled out in minutes. Amazingly, this man is recovering so well that after only

---

[220] John 17:12
[221] Romans 8:38–39

a week in the hospital, he's going home to finish his recovery. There is no doubt that the Father was leading and protecting this man. God is as involved and as powerful in our lives today as He was in Bible times, and He will continue to be so for all time. I hope you see God as a loving Father who is not just powerful over all things but as a personal leader to you.

Oftentimes we don't understand what God is doing. Why does God heal some people but not others? Why does He allow natural disasters and viruses to destroy people and places? Why does He not stop all of the bad things in the world? The truth is that we don't know. In Isaiah 55:8–9 says, "For my thoughts are not your thoughts, neither are my ways your ways, declares the LORD. For as the heavens are higher than the earth, so are my ways higher than your ways and my thoughts than your thoughts." But the Bible also assures us that as we suffer and struggle, God cares. He hears our cries for help and sees our tears. He alone knows exactly how far away this broken world is from the perfect one He originally made for us. When one of my children crashes on their bike and scrapes up their legs, I rush to help them with great compassion. How much more compassion and help does our heavenly Father have for us as we face struggles in life? We can't possibly understand all there is to know about God, the world, or His plan for it. But we can trust Him as the Leader of all things because He isn't just a leader; He's our Father. He loves us. He's all-powerful, and He's good.

We run into problems when we separate God's leadership from His goodness and his fatherhood. This is how we end up with a view of God as a faraway king issuing commands or moving us like chess pieces to satisfy His will. The truth is that God expresses his leadership to us primarily as our loving Father who wants relationship with us, wants to see us thrive, and invites us to join Him in all that He's doing in the world. How is your Father leading you today? What has He brought you through in the past year? What has He taught you about Himself? What has He begun to heal in you? God is always leading you and loving you. You just have to look.

Many of us did not have a dad who reflected God's loving, fatherly leadership. Instead we had a dad who didn't lead us, instruct us, or teach us a godly worldview. He was more like Adam than He was a reflection of the Father. This is a good time to remind you that God is a Father to the fatherless.[222] He Fathers you even if your dad didn't. His leadership means that He is in involved in every area of your life and not just for His own glory but in order to express His fierce, passionate love for you. If you had a weak dad who didn't lead, I want you to see that God is the strong Father you've always wanted. He uses His leadership to love and care for you.

Heavenly Father,
Thank you that I don't have to figure out life for myself.
I am so glad that you are in total control, that you love me,
and that I can trust your leadership in my life and in the world.
I pray that your Holy Spirit would fill me
and show me how you are leading me today.
Father, please show me my next step,
and the step after that, and after that,
until finally, one day, I am home with you.
In Jesus's name,
amen.

---

[222] Psalm 68:5

19

My Heavenly Father
Guides My Everyday Life

My dad didn't prepare me for adulthood.

I recently saw a T-shirt that said, "I don't want to adult today." *Adulting* is now an official word in the dictionary. It obviously means acting like an adult but especially doing those mundane things that we need to do but don't really want to do. This includes big things like sticking to a budget, filling out job applications, dumping the boyfriend that we know isn't good for us, yet also includes small things like laundry, paying bills, and going to the dentist. Who taught you to do these grown-up things? Hopefully, and ideally, the answer to this question should be, "My dad." Yes, moms are also involved in teaching kids how to become adults, especially little girls who will grow into women. I have three little girls, and they look up to me for a lot of things. But more and more, it's their daddy who is talking to them about life. Why do we serve others above ourselves? How do we act with people we know who don't go to church and don't know God? What should we do when we've wronged someone? How do we use our home, money, time, and talents God has given us to bless others?

Dads are a child's primary first interaction with someone who is "other." What I mean by that is when babies are little, they literally think they are the same person as Mom. That's how God designed things to work. Mom is usually the primary caregiver for a young child, but as that little one gets bigger, Dad is the first "other" person in a child's life. For better or worse, Dad is the first and primary link between the child and the world beyond the family.

That's how it was for the boy Jesus. Although Jesus retained His divine nature, He became fully human as well. Jesus grew in Mary's belly and began His human life as a tiny baby, just as we all do. As kids we had to learn, grow, and mature, and so did the boy Jesus. Luke 2:40 says, "And the child [Jesus] grew and became strong, filled with wisdom. And the favor of God was upon him." Jesus started his life on earth as a baby, then became a child, then a young man, then a mature man. He needed the tender love of his mom, Mary, but He also needed the guidance of His adopted earthly dad, Joseph, to help Him mature, just like regular people do.

Joseph reminds me of my father-in-law, Steve. Like Joseph, Steve is also a carpenter. He's been a homebuilder his whole life. And he would take my husband, Brandon, to work from the time that he was about ten years old. At that age young, Brandon was tasked with picking up the scraps of wood strewn about the jobsite. As Brandon got older, he learned how to do increasingly difficult tasks that required greater skill and maturity.

My husband learned much on that jobsite about working hard, managing the money that he earned, working with a team of people, and how to exercise wisdom to avoid getting hurt. One time, Steve showed Brandon the pay stub of one of his employees who had two children by two different mothers. Teenage Brandon stared in horror at the amount of money that was deducted from this man's hard-earned paycheck for child support and taxes. This man did have a responsibility to help support his children, but Brandon learned that he did not want to grow up to be a man who merely sent money to his children. He wanted to be a husband and father. Brandon spent many years working on jobsites with Steve, and all the while Steve sprinkled in timely life lessons, preparing his son for manhood. As a result of Steve's example of a good father, Brandon has never questioned that God is his Father who loves him and is on his side. Steve is like Joseph. He doesn't say a lot, but when he does it's important. He works hard, always providing for and leading his family. He's trustworthy, honest, and to this day, Steve is always available when Brandon needs him. God is a Father like that.

When we don't have a relationship with our earthly dad like Jesus or my husband did, it can have negative consequences as we grow into adults. Practically speaking, without preparation for becoming an adult and launching into the world, we can be totally be confused about what to do with our lives. This was me. The only thing I remember my dad saying to me in college was, "Don't major in art history." (I loved art history and still do.) But I didn't get any help in identifying my talents and abilities in making a plan to develop my skills and set goals. I didn't have the discipline to stick with any plan I would have made anyway. I just winged it. As you can imagine, and maybe identify with, having no plan didn't turn out very well. I went to a small liberal arts university, and upon graduating, I thought I'd "make a difference in the world" by going to Peru and helping farmers become more effective in their business. But that didn't feel right, so I thought I'd go to grad school, but I didn't want an additional $40,000 in student loans. Next, I explored cosmetology school, event planning, and culinary school. None of those were right either, so I just bounced around to different jobs. I worked at a bank, a mortgage company, a recruiting firm, and ended up as a nanny. There's nothing wrong with any of those jobs, but I was exhausted, directionless, and felt like I was wasting my young adulthood. I wanted to use my gifts and talents; I wanted to serve others, and I wanted to be challenged.

I'm not wholesale blaming my upbringing for my wandering as an adult, but it was a factor. Certainly, there are other people I could have sought out for wisdom and guidance, but I didn't. I can think of times when I knew something I was trying was fruitless, but I did it anyway. There were also times when I felt the Holy Spirit guiding me but I chose something else. What I am trying to do is illustrate an all-to-common, very real occurrence: when we don't receive guidance, develop discipline, and learn to rely on God the Father from our own dads, we can easily end up as grown-ups with adult-size freedom but child-size maturity. If our dad didn't guide us as we were growing up, we often don't even realize the God the Father is ready, willing, and able to guide us now.

Another reason that we may not understand how God guides and leads us in our life is quite simple and affects almost all of us—whether we had a godly dad or not. Life is just busy. School, work, children, church, appointments, relationships, home projects, vacations, the news... I could go on and on with all of the things that compete for our attention every single day. Sometimes I feel like life is a treadmill that keeps on going, and I'm trying to keep up so that I don't fall on my face. Or maybe a more accurate illustration is one of those circus acts where a clown is holding long poles with a spinning plate on the top of each one. He's got one pole in each hand, one on his foot, and one on his chin. Better keep those plates balanced and spinning or they'll all crash! The result is that we are so busy keeping pace with our life that we don't stop to experience God's presence and seek His guidance for the future. Instead of ordering our lives according to God's guidance, we allow our lives to control us.

Here, too, we can learn from the relationship that adult Jesus had with the Father. It was a normal occurrence for Jesus to "withdraw to desolate places and pray" to the Father. His life was busy! He traveled constantly, and his interactions with people swung like a pendulum—some groups loved him, others hated him. His life was much like ours: some miraculous things and a lot of mundane things. And just like Jesus, we need God the Father's presence to guide us through the craziness of life.

Now let's be honest for a minute. For many of us, our tendency is often to go to God for help only once something big hits. You have a crisis in a relationship. You lost your job. You want to find a husband but have only had a string of unpromising first dates while everyone around you is getting married and having babies. You want to start a business, go to school, or buy a house, but it feels like doors keep closing one after another. All are good times to reach out to God for help. All are times when we need to feel His presence and guidance in our lives.

But what about the little things? When you have a child who is struggling with the same thing day after day: when you're weary of doing the same tedious tasks every day—studying, mopping floors, commuting in traffic; when you scroll through social media and see what seems to be everyone else's exciting lives while yours feels stuck, God is with you in all of those small things too. His desire to guide us never wanes in our lives but rather is constant. Your heavenly Father is with you—to lead, guide, comfort, instruct you—every minute of every day. I know you've heard that before. Probably many times. But stop and really think about that. Whether a situation is big or small, the Father is with you and will guide you in whatever you need. Do you need wisdom? Do you need to make a big decision? Do you need comfort? Do you need self-control? God your Father is ready, willing, and able to give you whatever you need by the power of His Spirit. Just like Steve used to teach Brandon big life lessons in seemingly ordinary moments, the Father can use mundane moments to connect with us in a profound way. I'll show you what I mean.

My Father Watches Over Me

I had a spiritual experience while going to Costco yesterday. I left all my children at home with my husband. You moms understand what a miracle this is! But that wasn't why my Costco trip felt so supernatural, although that was a factor. In all seriousness, while I was walking into Costco, I thought of Job 34:21, which says, "For his eyes are on the way of a man, and he sees all his steps." Yes, God was with me and watching every single step of mine through Costco! Just that brief practice of stopping to remember this and to send up a prayer of thanks to God that I'm never alone (not even at boring ol' Costco!), completely changed my mundane chore into a time when I felt connection and closeness with the Father. And you know what? I felt more at peace after remembering that He was with me and watching me; it felt better than being alone. In fact, many years ago when I was just beginning to have babies, a wise older woman at church told me that it's crucial to "give your kids your eyes." When they wake up from a nap, when they get in the car after school, when they want to show you what they built with Legos, "give your kids your eyes." It communicates clearly that my heart is set on them, that I love them, that I am watching out for them. And it communicates to them that God is a Father whose loving eyes are always upon them. Your heavenly Father's eyes are upon you, and He sees all of your steps.

Sometimes we can slip into a belief that God is big and powerful and way up there in heaven. He's available if I need him, but He's busy doing "God things." This is a common misconception of God that many of us with distant dads struggle with. But the Bible tells us the opposite. God is not just available to you, but He also *chooses* to watch your every step, breath, and thought. Here are some additional Scriptures to help you remember throughout your day, whether it's full of the mundane or the miraculous, that God is your Father who watches over you:

> For the eyes of the LORD run to and fro throughout the whole earth, to give strong support to those whose hearts is blameless toward him. (2 Chron. 16:9)

> Behold, the eye of the LORD is on those who fear him, on those who hope in his steadfast love, that he may deliver their soul from death and keep them alive in famine. (Ps. 33:18–19)

> The eyes of the Lord are toward the righteous and his ears toward their cry. (Ps. 34:15)

> For a man's was are before the eye of the LORD, and he ponders all his paths. (Prov. 5:21)

> The eyes of the LORD are in every place, keeping watch on the evil and the good. (Prov. 15:3)

My Father Goes Before Me

In the closing chapters in the book of Deuteronomy, Moses was transitioning his leadership to Joshua. It would be Joshua, not

Moses, who would finally lead the Israelites into the promised land. (Moses would die before Israel crossed the Jordan into the promised land). Moses had been leading them for forty years ever since their escape from Egypt so this was a major transition for the people. Joshua was a much younger man than Moses, and they would have to trust him to lead them in battle against the current inhabitants of the land of Canaan. I'm sure they were afraid, and the future seemed uncertain. God lovingly reassured both the people and Joshua specifically (how big a responsibility he had!) that He would go out before them:

> The LORD your God himself will go over before you. He will destroy these nations before you, so that you shall dispossess them, and Joshua will go over at your head, as the LORD has spoken... It is the LORD who goes before you. He will be with you; he will not leave you or forsake you. Do not fear or be dismayed.[223]

God promised that He had been and would continue to care for Israel "just as a father cares for his child."[224] He would go before them. He would be the one to conquer the nations that stood before Israel. He had already carved the path for His people and destined them to live in a peaceful and prosperous place. All they needed to do was follow Him.

I can't tell you how many times in my life I remember this—that whatever happens in my day or in my life, God goes before me in love, protection, and guidance. With my loving Father leading the way, I am not alone. All I have to do is follow Him one step at a time. Now think about your own life:

> Before a job interview. Your Father goes before you.

---

[223] Deuteronomy 31:3, 8
[224] Deuteronomy 1:31

Before you have a difficult conversation with someone. Your Father goes before you.

Before you take a major test at school or in your career. Your Father goes before you.

Before your child throws a tantrum in the grocery store. Your Father goes before you.

Before you get bad report from the doctor. Your Father goes before you.

Before you get a phone call with tragic news. The Father goes before you.

Before _____.
Your Father goes before you.

You fill in the blank. Where in your life do you need to see that your loving Father goes before you? You do not have to be afraid of what may come. You do not have to worry that you're alone. Your heavenly Father is with you now, and He goes before you into the unknown. He wants to walk with you through every moment of every day because He loves you.

Heavenly Father,
Thank you that you love to watch over me
And that you go before me in all circumstances.
I pray that you'd send the Holy Spirit to remind me
every day, in every situation, that you are with me
and that you will guide my every step.
Please give me peace that comes from your presence
and confidence to face the future
because you are always with me.
In Jesus's name,
amen.

20

My Heavenly Father Has a Plan for the Whole World

My dad didn't have a plan for our family.

Alice's dad seemed like he knew what he was doing when it came to leading the family. They didn't have a lot of money for extra things like vacations or fancy cars, but they never seemed to lack anything they needed. She assumed, like most daughters, that her dad was planning for the future. But when the time came for her to go to college, she had to take out extensive student loans, which she was still paying nearly fifteen years after graduating. Alice's dad also didn't help her plan for her future practically. She had longed for her dad to talk, plan, and dream with her about what college majors or careers might fit with her interests and gifts. But he never did. It's not the years of student loan payments or the career changes that hurt, it's her dad's lack of involvement, the weak relationship. What bothers Alice the most is that he didn't care enough to have a plan for the future or for her.

In a previous chapter, we talked about how a dad is supposed to be the leader of the home and that he creates the home kingdom for better or worse. This is achieved both through what dad teaches and what he tolerates. In this way, a dad communicates to his children's beliefs, convictions, worldview, and direction in life. From this home environment, children learn what the goal of life is, for better or worse. Is the goal of life fortune? Fame? Family? Fruitfulness? Ideally, a dad creates a home culture that reflects God's kingdom culture and builds a strong, loving relationship in the home. From this, children learn something of what it is like to trust and love their Heavenly Father and his direction in their life.

As always, the good news is that God is a Father to the fatherless. He is a good Father who loves you deeply, passionately, and personally. And He is a Father with a plan. Now, we need to do a little theological heavy lifting before we can get on to some practical tips on how to live your life in accordance with God's plan. So, buckle up, but I promise it's important.

Way back in time, before God created the world we know, there was a war in heaven. Satan used to be an angel, but he rebelled against God, wanting to be the one in charge himself. As a result, God cast Satan out of heaven, and he took other fallen angels with him.[225] They are called demons. So today in the world, there are two teams. There is God's team and Satan's team. Satan lies through the culture of the world, trying to get people to believe that there are many perspectives, paths, and belief systems that are all equally valid. Satan loves to create gray areas and so deceive people. But the truth is that there is light, and there is dark. There is truth, and there are lies. There is life, and there is death. Two teams. This is why we have to be very careful about listening to teaching or teachers who are "spiritual." They may be believing very crafty, sneaky, seemingly innocuous schemes of Satan and his demons rather than the truth of God.

Although Satan certainly succeeds in deceiving some people into believing his lies, he is the most deceived of all. He believes he is right, and God is wrong. Yet there is absolutely no way that Satan or his demonic servants will win in the end against God. Jesus already defeated the power that the enemy has over us in the present by his death on the cross on our behalf. Jesus put Satan and his demons "to open shame by triumphing over them" through his life, death, burial, resurrection, and ascension back into glory in heaven.[226] Even better than that, when Jesus comes back again, he will send Satan and his

---

[225] Revelation 12:7–9
[226] See Colossians 2:15.

demons to the eternal torments of hell where they can never again hurt, harm, accuse, deceive, or lie to anyone ever again.

On the other hand, those of us to belong in God's family because of the work of Jesus have a much different destiny awaiting us. When God made the earth, He created a beautiful garden, set Adam and Eve in it, and gave them the job of ruling and enjoying the earth—making babies, exploring, settling in new territories, creating cities, establishing nations. God didn't abandon His plan for the earth and humanity just because Satan succeeded in twisting everything by tempting Adam and Eve to sin. No, Satan isn't that powerful. God's good plan that He set in motion in the Garden of Eden is still His plan. Except when Jesus comes back again, He won't just make things right. He'll make everything new *and* bring heaven with Him as well:

> "And I heard a loud voice from the throne saying, 'Behold, the dwelling place of God is with man. He will dwell with them, and they will be his people, and God himself with be with them as their God. He will wipe away every tear from their eyes, and death shall be no more, neither shall there be mourning nor crying nor pain anymore, for the former things have passed away… Behold, I am making all things new.'"[227]

Believe it or not, what we who belong to God have waiting for us is far better than simply returning to the perfection and beauty of Eden. There will be no more opportunity for sin, suffering, death, broken relationships, or fear to occur any longer. When Jesus brings the new heavens and the new earth, we will be perfected as well. We will still be ourselves; we will still have relationships; we'll still get to learn and explore and dream and design. We'll get to travel and make memories with those we love and even with God Himself, for we will live *with Him.*

---

[227] Revelation 21:3–5

I want you to use your imagination and begin to truly dream about what life in heaven with God will be like. Jesus said that we need to receive the kingdom of God like a child.[228] A few years ago, we went to Disneyland with our four children. The minute we told them we were going, the questions began. Can we see Disney Princesses? Can we buy some Mickey ears? Can we get ice cream and stay up late and go on lots of rides? Their excitement was infectious as their imaginations ran wild. They were planning and longing and counting down the days until we went on that trip.

Our desires and dreams of heaven are supposed to be like this. As I've been studying, I've given a lot of thought to what I want to do in heaven. I really want to take a walk with Jesus. I want to ask Him if I can rewatch the births of my four children. And I really want to see my great-grandparents, Wesley and Gladys, who were missionaries all over the world. I was young when they died, and I have loads of questions. I'm dying to meet Peter and Paul. I want to ask the women who found Jesus's empty tomb what that was like! And I want to travel to all the places in the world that are too expensive for me to travel to right now. I want to read books and cook meals and enjoy the beauty of God's world and His presence. Who do you want to see in heaven? What do you want to do in heaven? What do you want to learn in heaven? Really try to picture it in your mind's eye.

The Bible has a lot to say about what life will be like in eternity with God, you just have to be on the lookout for it. And from the picture that the Bible gives us, it is good for us to think about what we want to do when everything is made new and we are finally home with God because the more we think about it, the more we'll long for it.

So what does all this cosmic, spirit-realm talk mean practically for you and me? It means that we need to choose a side. First John 2:17 says, "And the world is passing away along with its desires, but whoever does the will of God abides forever." If we believe the things the world is teaching us about life (which ultimately come from Satan), we will waste our life. If we believe in God as our Father and

---

[228] Mark 10:15

seek His plan for life, we will invest our life for all eternity. Life is not about getting what we want, having our needs fulfilled, having all of the possessions we long for, having a perfect body, or getting recognition for our achievements. Life is also not ultimately about being kind, achieving unity in society, or working for social justice. Those are not ends in themselves; God and his kingdom are the end. Only then do we experience true kindness, unity, justice, and all the other things we long for. Our life is about loving God, learning what his kingdom is like, and living in such a way as to pull some of that kingdom down here to earth, hoping that other people will come to know, love, and follow the Father too.

As Christians, our citizenship is in heaven.[229] We will spend all of eternity in the presence of God in heaven, for that is our true home. However, our current residence is in the world. That means that our Father has placed us in our lives, these exact times and places,[230] as missionaries. I often hear people talk about being "on mission," like God has sent us for action. This isn't untrue, but I think He's primarily sent us to build relationships. First, we need to build our relationship with him. Then, we need to share his love with others. Jesus himself said as much:

> Jesus answered them, "This is the work of God, that you believe in him whom he has sent." (John 6:29)

> "Teacher, which is the greatest commandment in the Law?" Jesus replied: "'Love the Lord your God with all your heart and with all your soul and with all your mind.' This is the first and greatest commandment. And the second is like it: 'Love your neighbor as yourself.' All the Law and the Prophets hang on these two commandments." (Matt. 22:36–40)

---

[229] Philippians 3:20
[230] Acts 17:26

Jesus made it pretty clear that the point of the Christian life is to love God and show that love to others. But how? Jesus showed us that too. He was the only person who has perfectly lived as a citizen of heaven (that's where He was in eternity past and where He is today) and also a resident of Earth (where he lived for about thirty-three years), as a missionary of God's kingdom. Jesus repeatedly said the He came to carry out the Father's will and to show us what the Father is like. He is the only person who has ever or will ever live perfectly as a citizen of heaven and not been knocked off course by the world's culture. Jesus only and always lived for the Father's kingdom. How did He do it? How did He keep his heart, mind, and sights aligned with the kingdom and the Father's will while living in our fallen world? The answer is simple: He had a close relationship with His Father and continuously relied on the power of the Holy Spirit to walk in the Father's will. When we are close to the Father and receive His love, we will develop a heart like His, a heart like Jesus has. In addition, if we're willing, He'll show us ways we can bring a bit of his kingdom down into the world.

So does doing God's will and bringing His Kingdom into the world mean that we all follow some heavenly script? Does it mean I have to figure out the exact role I'm supposed to play or else I mess up my whole life? Not exactly. Some people view God's will like a single-lane country dirt road. There's one right way to go if you want to reach your destination. No diverting from the path or you'll end up in a ditch. God's will is actually much more like a multilane highway. There are many lanes you could choose, and they all go the same direction. They all end up at the same place. He's not looking for begrudging obedience to His will nor is His will some secret code that we need to crack. Most of the time, there are many ways, within the scope of your gifts, talents, opportunities, and resources to be obedient to God's will and to please Him. You can feel free to pick whichever lane you want, but you also need to make sure you're on the correct road and going in the right direction. We can't just do whatever we want and slap "in Jesus's name" or "for the glory of God" on the end of it and assume that means it is brought under the will of the Father. God doesn't bless *your* desires, ideas, and endeavors. He blesses *His*. And as we grow closer to Him, we want what He wants. The beauty of God's will is that we can do the things that He has planned for us in our own way, according to how He uniquely made us.

While we do have freedom in doing God's will in our lives, the things we do and the courses we take ought to be carefully and intentionally decided upon. Let's talk about some practical ways to help you figure out what God's will is in your life.

Principles

In discerning what God's will is for our life, the first place to go is the Bible. It is filled with principles, which are truths that apply to all times, places, and peoples. For example, we reap what we sow (Gal. 6:7). Liars will always be exposed because truth eventually comes to light (Prov. 12:19; Luke 8:17). The person who refuses to listen to correction brings harm to himself and will eventually do something stupid (Prov. 12:1). Oftentimes we like to cling to the promises of God more than the principles of God. His promises are true, but so are His principles. Pastor and author Charles Stanley says that principles "can be ignored but not broken."[231] We can sometimes prolong the effects, but God's principles always eventually prove true. Learning the principles of God and learning to live by them involves reading the Scriptures so as to renew our minds. Romans 12:1–2 (NIV) says, "Do not be conformed to the pattern of this world, but be transformed by the renewing of your mind. Then you will be able to test and approve what God's will is—His good, pleasing, and perfect will."

Prayer

During his Sermon on the Mount, Jesus taught the gathered crowds to pray like this: "Our Father in heaven, hallowed be your name. Your kingdom come, your will be done on earth as it is in

---

[231] Stanley, Charles. *The Spirit-Filled Life*, 245.

heaven."[232] Jesus came from heaven. He knew how amazing it was (and still is). He knew that the Father wanted only good for His children. So Jesus, our Big Brother taught us to pray: "Dad! Can you make the earth down here be more like it is up there?" Our only hope for improving this world comes from us looking up to heaven and asking our Father to bring some of His kingdom down here. We need kingdom love, kingdom peace, kingdom forgiveness, kingdom leadership, kingdom courage, kingdom faithfulness, and kingdom unity. None of those things can truly come from the world, only counterfeits come from the world.

Jesus prayed this prayer specifically for himself in the Garden of Gethsemane on the night before his crucifixion. Jesus was in anguish over what He knew was coming—the most brutal and shameful death imaginable and momentary broken relationship with his Father. And as Jesus unloaded all of his emotions onto the Father, He still prayed, "My Father, if it be possible, let this cup pass from me; nevertheless, not as I will, but as you will."[233] Jesus knew that his next step was going to be excruciatingly difficult, but He trusted in the Father's good, loving will. We need to follow Jesus's teaching and his example and pray, "Father, your will be done." Unwillingness to pray this prayer about a decision, an opportunity, or a relationship is an important indicator that you'd rather not know what God has to say about it. Been there done that. Don't feel bad if this is you. Just start by praying now.

Peace

Is there something you are considering or really have a passion to do, but as you think through all of the details, something doesn't sit well? Do you have peace about something even though others around you tell you you're wrong? Does what you want to do align with or conflict with the Bible? Maybe you know and have an inner peace about what God is asking you to do next but you're afraid to

---

[232] Matthew 6:9–10
[233] Matthew 26:39

do it. Or perhaps you just don't want to do it. "The absence or presence of peace is often the first indication that the Holy Spirit is up to something," explains Charles Stanley.[234] These are all helpful things to think and pray through when determining what your next step is.

Philippians 4:6–7 (NLT) says this, "Do not worry about anything; instead pray about everything. Tell God what you need, and thank him for what he has done. Then you will experience God's peace, which exceeds anything we can understand. His peace will guard your hearts and minds as you live in Christ Jesus." When you feel like worrying, pray instead. And this passage doesn't say that we'll get an answer to our specific prayer right away. Rather, we will get peace from God that will guard our hearts and minds so we can walk in obedience to what he's given us to do. The word "guard" in the original Greek has military connotations. Imagine a city surrounded by soldiers to keep the inhabitants safe inside and the enemies outside. The Father's peace guards you like that. His peace makes you safe and strong. Having peace about a situation doesn't necessarily mean it's God's will for you, but it is a key component of decision-making. Yet a lack of peace is definitely an indication to pump the breaks and learn more about a situation or opportunity before taking action.

People

The Bible tells us many times that advice from wise, godly people is crucially important when we are trying to make big decisions, process confusing emotions, and when we are in uncertain circumstances.

> Where there is no guidance, a people falls,
> but in an abundance of counselors there is safety.
> (Prov. 11:14)

> Without counsel plans fail, but with many
> advisers they succeed. (Prov. 15:22)

---

[234] Stanley, Charles. *The Spirit-Filled Life*, 209.

> For by wise guidance you can wage your
> war, and in an abundance of counselors there is
> victory. (Prov. 24:6)

Scripture tells us that wise counsel from people we trust brings us safety. When our emotions are running high, wise friends can help us make a clear-headed decision. Negative emotions, like fear, lead us to make bad choices. Other times, we can be so passionate about something that we lose sight of wisdom. Wise counsel can also help us think and pray through the details of situations or decisions so that we have a better chance at succeeding. Where two or three are gathered in the name of God, He promises to be there with them also.[235] Invite wise, godly people into your life, and let them pray with you and for you as you try to discern what God's will is for your life. And if you aren't willing to allow others to speak into your life, that can be a critical indicator that the path you're headed down might be the wrong one. There is a difference between keeping something private, between just a few other people and yourself, and keeping it completely to yourself.

Patience

Discerning what is in line with God's will is obviously important. But what is equally as important, and not often considered, is God's timing. I remember this feeling as a new wife. I wanted so badly to have a baby, but my husband wisely wanted to wait one year so we could get some financial things in order and adjust to being married. At the time, I was deeply frustrated. We knew we wanted to have a big family, so why the hold-up? I didn't understand that we shouldn't only follow God's will but also His timing. I was only considering what I wanted, but my husband was considering the financial, practical, and spiritual health of our future family. Turns out, my husband was right. We needed that year to get some things in order. And we had a great time just the two of us strength-

---

[235] Matthew 18:20

ening our new marriage. Ecclesiastes 3:1 says, "For everything there is a season, and a time for every matter under heaven." Our heavenly Father made the entire universe and keeps every molecule in perfect order simply by the power of his word. He has no beginning and no end. He is not bound by time as we are. He knows all things, and in Him all things hold together.[236] He loves you and wants good for you. So let's not only desire to do God's will but also trust in His perfect timing.

Small Things with Great Love

As I sometimes do (ahem), I'm going to get on a soapbox for a minute. You might disagree with me, but please hear me out before you decide. I often see books, media, and blogs that give what seems to be good advice. "Dream big! Set goals! Start that business! Write that book! Launch that blog! Pursue that opportunity! Increase your social media influence! Follow your dream!" Remember: God doesn't bless *your* desires; He blesses *His* desires. And His desires bless everyone! Maybe you should pursue that dream you have. But maybe you shouldn't. I don't know which is right for you. That's a conversation between you and the Lord and with wise people you trust. But I'll tell you what, it's not likely that we should pursue every dream we have because our hearts can deceive us.[237] It's also not likely that we'll all find extraordinary success in our endeavors. If you pursue the wrong thing, or even the right thing at the wrong time, you can waste a lot of time and resources.

I realize this sounds like a hypocritical thing to say coming from someone who pursued my dream of writing a book. However, I will tell you that that the process was nothing like I wanted it to be and everything that God wanted it to be. Many times I'd sit down to write and have no clue how to begin, so I prayed and waited until He gave me direction. Other times, I felt that I was ready to pursue publishing and it was very clear that it was not yet

---

[236] Colossians 1:17
[237] Jeremiah 17:9

God's time for that. So I waited. And in the waiting, God changed, grew, and purified my heart in more ways than I could have ever anticipated. While this project took much longer than I originally wanted, I now see and am thankful for God's perfect timing. I did not follow God's leading perfectly, and there were times I really struggled to get onboard with His plan, but I'm here to tell you from actual lived experience that God's way *and* His timing are always, always the best.

It is also true that you don't have to do "big" things to make a big impact. There is no one who will have the same kind of influence in the lives of those closest to you than *you*. No one will influence your husband or your kids or your best friend like you can. No one will love and honor your aging parents like you will. No one else has ever invited your coworker to church, but you can. God placed specific people in your life so you can share His love in a way that is unique to them. Having "influence" to an audience of clients, customers, or a community online isn't necessarily bad. But it's not for everyone. Please do not let the values of the world's culture or the contagion of the latest trends overshadow the ministry opportunities that your heavenly Father has placed right in front of you.

Let me give you an example. You may have heard this quote by Mother Theresa: "Do small things with great love." Not surprisingly in our fast-paced world with soundbites and tweets, that quote is taken out of context. The entire quote is "*We cannot all do great things*. But we can do small things with great love (emphasis mine)." You might be thinking, "Well, that's a terrible example. Mother Theresa is, well... MOTHER THERESA!" However, she wasn't always a famous, revered saint.

In 1928, Mother Theresa left her home in Albania at the age of eighteen and moved to Ireland to learn English and become a missionary. She arrived in India a year later. She became a teacher at a school and later served as its headmistress for nearly twenty years. Mother Theresa later opened the Missionaries of Charity. In her words, it would be a place where she and her helpers would care for "the hungry, the naked, the homeless, the crippled, the blind, the lepers, all those people who feel unwanted, unloved, uncared for throughout society, people that have become a burden to the society and are shunned by everyone."[238] Mother Theresa served the poor, the sick, and the dying. Not a glamorous job by a longshot. She fed them, clothed them, and comforted them. She gave them safe places to stay and loving places to die. She dressed simply—in a white cotton sari with a blue border—and lived a humble, loving life of service to the Lord and to those who no one else wanted to help. Mother Theresa didn't do "great" things by the world's standards. She didn't own a multimillion-dollar company, drive a fancy car, or live in a mansion. She didn't wear designer clothes or keep up with the latest beauty trends. No, she simply did countless little things with great love, faithfulness, and humility out of her love for God and others.

Her life shows us what we ought to do as well. Serve those that God places in front of us. Do the next thing we know how to do. Continue to do what we know, step after step, for the rest of our lives. Eugene Peterson calls this "long obedience in one direction." Mother Theresa also shows us the exceeding impact we can make simply by showing others the ministry of presence. When we sit with someone, pray with them, listen to them, literally just be with them and spend time with them, we are reflecting to them something of the everywhere, always loving presence of God. Some of us will indeed do "big things" for God, but all of us have the opportunity to do small things with great love. And here's the ironic thing: it's often the "little things" that matter the most to someone. Your Father doesn't measure "big" or "small." Your job is simply to share the love that you've received from Him with a world that desperately needs it. The best plan for your life is God's plan for your life.

---

[238] https://www.washingtonpost.com/wp-srv/inatl/longterm/teresa/stories/words.htm?noredirect=on

Heavenly Father,
I thank you that you have a plan
for this often sad, confusing, troubled world.
I praise you that I can play a part
in bringing a little bit of your kingdom down to earth.
Please give me guidance and peace to know
the next step you'd have me take.
May the Holy Spirit fill me and give me peace
As I wait with joy for the returning of your Son.
In Jesus's name,
amen.

21

My Heavenly Father Provides for All My Needs

My dad didn't provide for me.

If you ask just about any man what the primary roles of a father are, most will name provider at or near the top of the list. This is something that is built into God's design of family yet is being increasingly abdicated by dads in America today. For those of us who had a father who provided, we may not have worried that we wouldn't have our needs provided for. But for those who didn't have a dad who provided, worrying about our needs can still be a source of near-constant anxiety. Let's look at the stories of four different women and how they experienced a dad who didn't provide as well as how this affected their view of God.

While she was growing up, Emily's home was a warm, loving place. She lived with her dad, mom, and siblings. They all got along relatively well. Yet they always struggled to make ends meet. Her dad worked as hard as he could at a blue-collar job. Sometimes he even juggled multiple jobs. Emily's mom was a wise spender and stewarded what little money they had very well. Yet the mail was frequently full of past-due notices and credit card bills. Their electricity had even been shut off at one point. Some of Emily's earliest and most vivid memories are of being teased at school for her secondhand clothes and her worn-out shoes. None of the other kids knew how deep of a wound they had touched. Emily loved her dad and knew that he worked as hard as he could, but it never seemed to be enough. They were barely getting by. Even though Emily's dad really did try his best to provide for the family, she resented him for the family's constant struggles. She came to believe that God also wasn't able to take care of her, and so she had better take care of herself. Emily started working and making her own money as soon as she was able. She decided the best way to live her life was to be self-sufficient and not need help from anyone. She sought a career that would not only secure a good income but also garner respect and notoriety. She wanted to prove to herself (and everyone else) that she was better than the poor upbringing she came from.

Karen's family also looked normal from the outside. Actually, they looked like they were thriving. Her dad had a great career and was able to buy many expensive things—houses, cars, boats, jet skis, and vacations. He also had many hobbies—golf, skiing, and motorcycles, to name a few. He had a penchant for "big-boy toys." Whenever the latest iPhone came out, you can bet that Karen's dad was one of the first people to get one. Karen's dad was all about having a good time. But he didn't think into the future. He didn't have a long view of his financial success. Instead of investing some of his income for the future and wellbeing of his family, he spent it all. Karen's dad did not know the meaning of delayed gratification. Whatever he wanted, he got. Yet if Karen asked her dad to spend some quality time with her, he would say he was too busy—either with work (where did she think all that money came from, after all?) or with his own recreational activities. All she wanted was to spend time with her dad; she didn't care about the flashy things his money could buy. As a result, Karen says she began to resent her dad and began to view God in a similar way. She began to believe that He, too, was a shortsighted, capricious God who was too busy gratifying his own desires to pay attention to her.

Susan's dad moved out of the house when she was three years old. Though her parents were divorced, her dad did have visitation privileges. However, he rarely exercised them, and the roles of both mom and dad were left to Susan's mom to fulfill. Her mom was kind, loving, attentive, and had a job that provided well for Susan and her younger brother. Her material needs were always met. In fact, her material "wants" were always met too. Susan's mom had a successful career so they had a nice house and car, went to private school, took vacations, and played sports. Susan's mom provided everything. They didn't receive child-support checks from her dad (although he was supposed to pay), but he would send Christmas and birthday gifts on occasion. Susan remembers one Christmas in particular. Though Susan's dad lived only a short drive away, he sent her Christmas gift to her house in the backseat of an empty taxi. Not surprisingly, Susan grew up to believe that God was able to provide for her and have a relationship with her; He just didn't want to.

Jennifer's parents were divorced. On paper, things looked like they had been sorted out. Jennifer's mom retained full custody of her while her dad moved out of state and made regular child-support payments. In fact, he never missed one. All of her material and physical needs were provided for her. However, what Jennifer wanted more than her dad's money was a relationship with him. In fact, without the relationship, the money didn't mean very much. She would have traded her dad's money for a relationship with him in a heartbeat. Jennifer came to believe that God was like a distant dad who would take care of her needs but didn't care to be connected with her or be part of her daily life.

Can you relate to any of these women? In your mind, is God a father like Emily's who is *limited* in his ability to provide for you? Or is he a father, like Karen's and Susan's, who is *unwilling* to provide for you? Perhaps you think He is a Father like Jennifer's who will provide for you but doesn't want a relationship with you. Be honest. When a need arises in your life that makes you anxious—you need to find a job, you aren't sure the right decision to make, or a situation seems too complicated for you to figure out—do you trust that God will provide what you need? How many things are you worrying about or feeling anxious about right now? What in your life feels beyond your control right now? What is causing you stress right now? Chances are, you *want* to trust your Father with these things, but maybe you don't know how.

Life Is More Than Dinner and Shopping

In Jesus's first recorded teachings of his earthly ministry, He instructs his disciples and the onlooking crowds about how to address the needs of our daily lives. In Matthew 6:25, Jesus commands, "Do not be anxious about your life, what you will eat or what you will drink, nor about your body, what you will put on." This seems like a mere command that we are to obey. Yet as we will see when Jesus continues, God never gives rules to us outside of the context of His relationship with us.

First Jesus says, "Is not life more than food, and the body more than clothing?"[239] The urgent little fires that pop up in life occupy so much of our time that they often become all we see. Did I pay the mortgage? What time do I need to get the kids at school? What are we having for dinner? I need to return that call or that email. I have to get gas, do laundry, track my order that is late. What should I wear today? I really need to get my hair cut and my nails done. The enemy loves to keep us busy and to keep our minds occupied with things that really aren't a big deal. Don't get me wrong. I love to put on a cute outfit and shoes. I am a nerd about skincare, nutrition, fitness, and the like. I know that all of the little things on our to-do lists need to get done. I also know that the bigger things in life—sickness, broken relationships, past hurts—are important and impactful. However, Jesus is telling us that in the scheme of eternity, as beings who will live forever—either in heaven with God or apart from Him forever in the torment of hell—we can't afford to let those lesser things crowd out eternal things. We must tend to the health of the inner life of our soul as well, or we will tap out. We'll fall and fail in the face of temptation, stress, fear, and spiritual unhealth.

So let's stop for a minute and ask ourselves some important questions: How is my soul? Am I thriving or am I withering? How is my time with God in His Word? How is my time talking with Him in prayer? We have to tend to the most important things of life first. Nothing is more important than the health of your soul and your relationship with the One who nourishes it. If we don't pay attention to our spiritual needs as well as our material needs, the material needs will count for nothing.

---

[239] Matthew 6:25

You Matter More Than Birds and Flowers

Another reason that Jesus gives for not being preoccupied with the material things of life is that we are valuable to God:

> Look at the birds of the air: they neither sow nor reap nor gather into barns, and yet *your heavenly Father feeds them. Are you not of more value than they?* ...And why are you anxious about clothing? Consider the lilies of the field, how they grow: they neither toil nor spin, yet I tell you, even Solomon in all his glory was not arrayed like one of these. But if God so clothes the grass of the field, which today is alive and tomorrow is thrown into the oven, will he not much more clothe you, O you of little faith?[240]

From eagles to barn owls, from hummingbirds to sparrows, all the birds of the earth are seen and fed by the Father. Flowers that are in the far corners of the world, unseen by human eyes, are made beautiful under the creative, watchful eye of the Father. We seem to think that creation hums along on autopilot, but it doesn't. The reason that the mountains don't fall into the sea or that the earth doesn't spin out of the sun's orbit is by the will of God. Are you more valuable than the animals and plants, planets and stars He so tenderly cares for? Of course you are! In all of creation, only people are made in His image. Only people have a soul that will live forever. Only people are called His beloved children and redeemed by the sacrifice of God's only Son. We know this in our minds, but sometimes we need to stop and remember it, and feel it in our hearts. You matter so much to your Father that He made every detail of you, loves you, and provides everything you need—food, shelter, friends, salvation, guidance, wisdom, protection... I could go on and on.

---

[240] Matthew 6:26, 28–30, emphasis mine

Now might be a good time to take a moment and make a list of all the things your Father has given you and to thank Him. Maybe write it in a journal, keep a note in your phone, or even jot it down right here in the margins of this book. Make your list somewhere that you will see it and remember how loved you are. To your Father, you are immeasurably more precious than the birds of the air and more beautiful than the lilies of the field.

Worry Doesn't Help

Another reason Jesus gives for us to not be anxious about our everyday needs is pretty simple: worrying doesn't help. "And which of you by being anxious can add a single hour to his span of life?"[241] Worry doesn't help a situation at all. We just get worked up and more anxious. We do not think clearly when we are anxious. Worry usually makes us focus on ourselves and what we cannot do, rather than on God and what He can do. Worry usually stems from fear and lack of control. Pastor and author Tim Keller explains worry this way: "When we worry, we are saying, 'I know the way my life is supposed to go, and God's not getting it right.'"[242]

Jesus went even farther than saying that worry is pointless; He said that *unbelievers* worry about what to eat and what to wear. The implication is that if we worry about these things as well, how are we different from them? What difference does knowing and belonging to God make in our everyday life? People who do not know God as their Father live their lives according to the world's rules and systems. According to the world's culture, you only have what you can earn or acquire yourself, and once you have something, you need to hang on to it before someone tries to take it. The world's culture is one of scarcity, coveting, stealing, and taking. Jesus says that God is your Father, and you don't need to worry like non-Christians do because your Father is a giver. He loves to give. He loves to provide. He loves to take care of you, and He has an endless supply from which to give. Jesus even said,

---

[241] Matthew 6:27
[242] https://www.azquotes.com/quote/1246588

"Your Father knows what you need before you ask him."[243] Think of that! Not only is God *able* to provide for you but also He *wants* to provide for you. God the Father is a dad who pays attention to the specific needs of each of his unique children and asks, "How can I help?"

Break the (World's) Rules

Let me remind you: this world is not your true home if you belong to God. I don't know about you, but I'm pretty happy about that. I suffer from terrible allergies—trees, grasses, dust, pollen, you name it. I'm basically allergic to nature. I'm also allergic to gluten, which, as my husband says, is what all delicious food is made of. When I get to heaven, I am going to breathe fresh air and eat croissants every morning for breakfast, and I'm really happy about it. We talked about our future with God at great lengths in the previous chapter—what it will be like to be in heaven, to see Jesus's face, to have no more problems or pain. While all of that is true, it is also true that your eternal kingdom life starts the moment you meet Jesus and are adopted into God's family. What that means is you do not have to play by the world's rules. You do not have to listen to the world's demands or standards or lies. The world or your circumstances do not dictate how you live. Jesus said, "But seek first the kingdom of God and his righteousness, and all these things will be added to you."[244] When I say *kingdom*, I mean the way that God intended life to be on earth and the way it always has been in heaven and the way it will be when Jesus comes back to make the world new: a place of love, joy, kindness, safety, relationship, and unity under God's perfect rule. A place without Satan, sin, death, disease, folly, pain, or division. So what did Jesus mean by saying "seek first the kingdom of God"? What does that look like in our lives?

Seeking God's kingdom means that we don't worship money, sex, food, success, or power like the world does. Instead we receive and enjoy them as gifts from the Father. Seeking God's kingdom

---

[243] Matthew 6:8
[244] Matthew 6:33

means that we don't use people to meet our own needs. Instead we love and serve them with the Father's love. Seeking God's kingdom means we don't need to worry about things like our appearance, our status, or what others think of us. Instead we live as beloved daughters of the most loving, kind, safe, joyful, faithful Father in the universe. We live with Jesus's return and the new heavens and new earth on the horizon as our final destination.

The world's culture is like a tidal wave, moving in the wrong direction in absolutely every way. Values are ever-changing. People seek to share their perspective rather than seek God's truth. Most people look out only for themselves rather than loving God and others. Hollow praise and affirmation seek to bring what only the healing love of God can. People hurl mean attacks at one another in order to feel better about themselves. And you will find yourself swept up in culture's tidal wave unless you actively seek to live by God's kingdom ways. How do we do this? The apostle Paul tells us:

> If then you have been raised with Christ, seek the things that are above, where Christ is, seated at the right hand of God [the Father]. Set your minds on things that are above, not on things that are on earth. For you have died, and your life is hidden with Christ in God. When Christ, who is your life appears, then you also will appear with him in glory.[245]

Your eternal life starts the moment you meet Jesus and are forgiven of your sin. You belong to your Father and are a member of his family, a citizen of his eternal kingdom. Though your current residence is in this broken world, the world will not stay broken. It—and you—will be made new and will live in the presence of the LORD forever! So set your heart and your mind on things above, on things that will outlast this world. The only things you'll take with you into the glory of eternity are your relationships and your mem-

---

[245] Colossians 3:1–4

ories. I'm not saying to ignore this life. We need to pay bills, raise our kids, go to work, and take care of our health. It is good to make memories with the people we love, to enjoy God's creation, and to spread the Good News of Jesus far and wide. But what I am saying is to not waste this life worrying about things that won't matter in the end. Your Father knows what you need before you even ask Him. He's taken care of your biggest need, forgiveness of your sin, and the destiny of your soul, so He will surely take care of everything else.

So don't waste your life. Invest it. Tell people about the love, forgiveness, and peace available to them through the work of Jesus on the cross. Tell them about the Father and how much He loves them and is eager for them to join His family. Tell them about the Holy Spirit, the very Spirit that raised Jesus from the dead, and how He lives in you and empowers you. Live a life that doesn't follow the world's rules. Live a life that follows kingdom rules. Show the people watching you that the one true kingdom belongs to your Father. Show them that it is a kingdom of love, safety, abundance, provision, joy, fun, life, and peace. And only this kingdom will have no end. When your life on this earth is done, you'll close your eyes to this world and open them to see your Big Brother Jesus welcoming you home into your Father's house. Do not be anxious, friend. For this is your destiny. Amen. Come, Lord Jesus!

Heavenly Father,
I confess that I often worry about the details of life.
Thank you for all the ways you've provided for me.
Please help me to trust you
and to show those around me
that you are a Father who loves to give.
Thank you for the ultimate gift
of salvation through Jesus.
Holy Spirit, help me to seek the kingdom.
In Jesus's name,
Amen.

Conclusion

I am so thankful that you have begun this journey to learn more about God the Father and to grow closer to Him. I hope and pray that who you were when you began reading this book is not who you are as you finish this book. My hope is not in anything that I have written but only in who He is and the Word He's given to us. I also want to exhort you to not just read this book and put it down, especially if you feel the Holy Spirit stirring in you that there is more healing to be had, more forgiveness to extend, and more growth to be experienced. You might want to read this book again, allowing God to dig a little deeper into your heart the second time around. Perhaps as you made your way through this book, you thought of other women who need to meet their heavenly Father and you can pass it on to them.

You may also want to talk about what you are thinking and feeling with a wise and trusted friend, a professional counselor, or a pastor. Having a safe and trustworthy person with whom to process your past, your pain, and new things you are learning can be very helpful. If possible, you may even want to have a conversation with your dad. I would encourage you to pray and ask God if this is a good option for you and to release any expectations that you might have about the outcome. Maybe such a conversation will be the beginning of healing and reconciliation for your relationship. On the other hand, I know women who have had conversations with their dad who helped them learn more about him but didn't necessarily help their relationship. Nevertheless, the conversations did help these women to grow in their relationship with God and continue to heal and forgive.

What I'm trying to say is, this is: please do not just read this book and put it on your shelf to collect dust. Please continue to get to know your heavenly Father, feel His healing love, forgive your dad, and help other women to do the same.

First John 3:2 says, "Beloved, we are God's children now, and what we will be has not yet appeared; but we know that when he appears we shall be like him, because we shall see him as he is." You are God's child *now*. Furthermore, who you are now is not who were and not who you will be when He is done with you. The Dad you have longed for is the Dad you have had all along and the One you will have for all time. Let's help one another to keep going until we're home with Him.